Marolyn
Psa 11:1

Walking
and
Talking
with
Jesus!

by
Marolyn Ford

Walking and Talking With Jesus,

©1993 by Full Court Press

P.O. Box 141513
Grand Rapids, Michigan 49514.

This book is available in quantity at special discounts for your group or organization. For further information contact:

Full Court Press
P.O. Box 141513
Grand Rapids, MI 49514

1 2 3 4 5 6 / 97 96 95 94 93
Printed in the United States of America

Table of Contents

Dedication

This book is affectionately and gratefully dedicated to my wonderful Savior, the Lord Jesus Christ, Who so graciously gave me the miracle of sight and to my husband, Acie, who shared in my years of blindness and with whom I now minister of Him who said: "I am the Light of the world!" (John 8:12).

Foreword

ENCOURAGEMENT in walking tall for Jesus and learning to experience Him as the ". . . friend who sticks closer than a brother" (Proverbs 18:24), is the thrust of this latest book from Marolyn Ford. Building an intimate relationship with Jesus Christ is essential in the development of the Christian life. A margin note in the New American Standard Version says that the word "friend" in Proverbs 18:24 carries the meaning of "lover." It is this expanding love relationship with Jesus that Marolyn shares with her readers.

Shortly after graduating from high school, Marolyn, who had learned many lessons in how to grow up in Jesus from her Christian parents, was stricken with blindness. This life-shattering experience which lasted thirteen years was used of the Lord to tenderly draw her more closely to Him. Marolyn's refuge during those years of darkness was to be found in Jesus, the lover of her soul.

As quickly as the blindness had overtaken her, God in His rich mercy and grace, restored her sight. The years that have followed Marolyn's "miracle," have been spent in sharing the marvelous grace of her loving Lord with thousands around the world.

Walking and Talking with Jesus will greatly enrich the lives of all who read it. And in the process, readers will learn and experience a deeper, more intimate relationship with the Lord Jesus Christ.

Several lines from the chorus of *It Is No Secret* by Stuart Hamblen say: "It is no secret, what God can do; what He's done for others, He'll do for you." Marolyn is one of God's "others." What God has done for Marolyn, He'll surely do for you.

I commend *Walking and Talking with Jesus* for your spiritual blessing in your Christian pilgrimage with Jesus.

Adrian Rogers
Memphis, Tennessee

About the Author

Marolyn shares her story with thousands each year across the United States as well as in foreign countries. After thirteen years of blindness the Lord miraculously restored her eye-sight through the prayers of her husband, Acie, and his faith in God's ability to do so. Marolyn is the author of *These Blind Eye's Now See.*

Recommending this book, Dale Evans Rogers writes, *"These Blind Eye's Now See* is a MUST. . . Marolyn Ford is a tremendous inspiration to all she meets, and is LIVING PROOF of the power of Jesus Christ to restore that which was lost — and use that restoration to His glory."

Marolyn is much in demand as a public speaker in crusades, conferences, conventions, seminars, civic clubs, and church meetings. In these appearances, she not only shares the testimony of her "miracle," but also speaks on many other topics.

She has also been interviewed on numerous TV programs, including several interviews on the 700 Club with Pat Robertson and Sheila Walsh. The CBN Network has produced a motion picture presentation titled "No Earthly Reason" based on Marolyn's life story called "Blind Love."

Marolyn is the wife of Acie L. Ford, Associate Pastor of the Broadmoor Baptist Church in Memphis, Tennessee. The Ford's daughter, Sharon, is a university student.

Arrangements to have Marolyn come and speak to your group can be arranged by writing or calling:

Marolyn Ford
c/o Broadmoor Baptist Church
3824 Austin Peay Highway
Memphis, Tennessee 38128
Church: 901/386-9643 or Home: 901/372-7647

Author's Preface

ACROSS THE YEARS of my journey with Jesus, He has taught me many lessons about the absolute importance of walking and talking with Him. Since I first trusted Him to be my personal Savior as a little girl, He has been at work in my life, developing a lifetime of companionship and fellowship.

I often recall the Scripture concerning Enoch. "Enoch walked with God; then he was no more, because God took him away" (Genesis 5:24/NIV). Too, I am reminded of the tremendous fellowship Adam and Eve enjoyed with God as I read, "Then the man and his wife heard the sound of the Lord God as he was walking in the garden in the cool of the day. . ." (Genesis 3:8a/NIV).

This precious fellowship with the Lord, walking and talking with Him, has characterized His people down through the ages. Though some of us have had the privilege of this fellowship for a longer period of time, yet the words of the chorus by John Stallings expresses it best:

Learning to lean, learning to lean,
I'm learning to lean on Jesus.
Finding more power than I'd ever dreamed,
I'm learning to lean on Jesus.

My purpose in this book, *Walking and Talking with Jesus,* is to share my experiences with you in the hope that you will join with me in *Learning to Lean* on Him!

Marolyn Ford
Memphis, Tennessee

xiii

Chapter One

Building Faith Before Tragedy

SITTING ON THE GREEN LAWN at the end of the day, looking across the acres of land, crops ripe unto harvest, green trees and blue skies, my heart welled up within me in adoration and praise to my Lord and Savior. As I lingered there in the spirit of prayer, I said so often, "Lord, I'm just a little country girl but somehow I pray that you will take my life and use it to point souls to the Lord Jesus Christ."

Living and working on a farm taught me a great deal about responsibility. Looking back, it was my preparation time for the tragedy of thirteen years of blindness which would come into my life when I became a young woman. I was never allowed to start a job without carrying it through to completion. Whether it was gathering eggs or planting a field, I finished the job with no thought about quitting. Even as a small child coloring in a coloring book, my mother would not allow me to leave one page unfinished to go to another. I learned responsibility and stick-to-it-iveness by practicing what was right.

God worked many things in my life during my growing-up years on the farm. I enjoyed the smell of a freshly plowed field. I loved to work in the fields; hauling in the bales of hay, cultivating the rows of young corn, working with the self-propelled combine and hauling the wheat crops into the barn. Often as I drove the John Deere tractor across the fields I sang. Oh, how I loved to sing songs about my Jesus at the top of my voice so I could hear myself over the noise of the tractor. I loved the farm and God's open air.

Family devotions were held at each meal. Around the table, we children were taught to read the Bible and pray. One evening, it was my turn to read. The passage was John, chapter three, verses one through thirty-six. As I read verses 16-18, "For God so loved the world that He gave His only begotten Son, that whosoever believeth in Him should not perish, but have everlasting life. For God sent not His son into the world to condemn the world; but that the world through Him might be saved. He that believeth on Him is not condemned; but he that believeth not is condemned already, because he hath not believed in the name of the only begotten Son of God" (KJ), my Dad began asking me thought provoking questions, difficult for a little girl to answer.

One question was, "According to what you've just read, are you condemned or are you not condemned?" As I wanted to answer correctly because my older brothers were sitting there listening, I reread it twice so I could comprehend it. I did want my answer to please my brothers and my Dad. I proudly answered, "I am not condemned." "How do you know?" Dad asked. I said, "Because it said that if I believe Jesus died and rose again from the dead for me, then I am not condemned. Because I have asked Jesus into my heart."

The dominant factor in forming my faith during my younger years, I believe, was this practice of my parents having family devotions. We gave thanks to the Lord in prayer before meals; then after we finished eating we read the Bible and prayed again. Though this time was short and to the point, each of us children learned the importance of the Word of God and prayer through our participation in reading and praying.

The family altar can be a time to teach children to build the qualities of "gold, silver and precious stones" into their lives. It teaches them to worship and honor the Lord as King of Kings; to depend upon the Lord for emotional, physical, spiritual and practical needs. It can also be a time for singing and praising the Lord.

Personal God-Consciousness Restrains Sin

Having been active daily in personal, private and family devotions to God, I learned to feel an extreme God consciousness and developed a strong, keen desire to walk with the Lord. His presence had overshadowed me. My spirit became sensitive about not grieving the Holy Spirit or walking in any form of disobedience. The questionable pleasures many teenagers enjoyed were not a part of my life. Places where most teenagers felt comfortable, I did not. I was constrained to draw back from anything that was worldly or impure.

As an example, I remember so vividly a particular restaurant where many of my schoolmates went daily for lunch. My twin sister, Carolyn Black, and I went in one day at lunch time. The music was loud and the decor was dark (not that there is anything wrong with loud music or dark decor). Somehow, the presence of evil surrounded us. We could not stay for lunch in a place where I knew God was uncomfortable. It was "off limits" for us. The Holy Spirit would not allow us to eat there. I diligently practiced keeping my mind on God, His thoughts, His will and way. And when something was not pleasing to God, I knew it.

Pray Without Ceasing

The element in my life that prepared me for thirteen years of blindness was the development of continual prayer. However, it is important, not only to bring our petitions to Him, but also to take the time to listen to what He wants to say to us. Our needs and desires are not nearly as important as listening to Him. God speaks to us in our spirit through the written Word. It is vital that we listen to Him.

I remember learning the power of praying in my spirit when playing in my room as a child. No one was there but the Lord and me. I was singing the song, *Cleanse Me.* I've included the words here so you can think and meditate on them. Allow the Holy Spirit to grip your spirit through them as He did mine.

Cleanse Me

Search me, O God, and know my heart today;
Try me, O Savior, know my thoughts, I pray.
See if there be some wicked way in me;
Cleanse me from every sin, and set me free.
I praise Thee, Lord, for cleansing me from sin;
Fulfill Thy Word and make me pure within.
Fill me with fire, where once I burned with
shame;
Grant my desire to magnify Thy name.

Lord, take my life, and make it wholly Thine;
Fill my poor heart with Thy great love divine.
Take all my will, my passion, self, and pride;
I now surrender, Lord — in me abide.

O Holy Ghost, revival comes from Thee;
Send a revival, start the work in me.
Thy Word declares Thou wilt supply our need;
For blessing now, O Lord, I humbly plead.

I must have sung it more than fifty times. Each
time, I realized a little bit more how I could not
face God with any sin in my life. Sin must be dealt
with immediately, not later. Short accounts must
be kept with God. Failure to confess sin would
bring the loss of confidence gained when walking
with Him. With unconfessed sin in our lives, we
cannot come into His presence with boldness and
expect to receive anything. Why choose to be
powerless when we can be so powerful?

My heart was deeply touched by the soul-
searching words of this song. In the stillness of
the hour, I was brought before God. With these

words burning in my heart, I learned to walk the road of total commitment. More than anything, I wanted my life to count for Jesus Christ. Years later, the words of this song still penetrate my very soul.

I know there are many to whom God's Word is dead. Though they read it the Holy Spirit has not quickened it (made it alive) to them. They are just dead words. But to me, it has always been alive and living within me. Since my coming to Christ for salvation, I ever thirst for more and more of Him and His Word.

Paul instructed Timothy, "What I am eager for is that all the Christians there will be filled with love, that comes from pure hearts, and that their minds will be clean and their faith strong" (I Timothy 1:5). Service to God is to be from a pure heart, a clean mind and a strong faith. I always sensed a God-given restraint to keep me from sin. I knew that which pleased the Lord and that which did not. My conscience was tender. Consequently, it had a strong effect upon what I did and where I went.

Prayer meetings on Saturday's and sing-spirations with the church group were my joy and delight. I felt and understood the presence of God in my life. Learning about His power was a growing experience. I knew forgiveness and obedient living. Obedience to the promptings of the Spirit is essential to having the blessing of God. I knew that I could not approach the presence of God while living in disobedience to the Holy Spirit because God cannot look upon sin. I found the closer I came to God the more terrible the least of my sins became. The Spirit of God, His presence and the manifestation of His divine power held me close to the Lord and still does today.

God Prepares Us Before Tragedy Strikes

I know that I would never have been able to handle blindness as a young girl if God had not prepared me from the very beginning. Of course, there were many lessons yet to come which God would teach me along the way. The words of an old chorus which we sang at singspirations have helped me.

> Only to be what He wants me to be,
> Every moment of every day.
> Yielded completely to Jesus alone,
> Every step of this pilgrim way.
> Just to be clay in the Potter's hands,
> Ready to do what His will commands.
> Only to be what He wants me to be,
> Every moment of every day.
> — Norman J. Clayton

Eighteen years of age and blind. Before me was college, a career, marriage. And who would marry a blind girl? I thought my life was completely shattered as it crumbled at my feet.

For weeks after I became blind, I sat for hours in my Dad's easy chair and listened to sacred gospel records. I sank my soul into the music as it lifted my thoughts heavenward. I felt the comforting presence of the Holy Spirit surrounding me. The words of the songs lifted my thoughts in prayer and praise to the Lord Jesus. In this way, I kept my mind off myself and my insurmountable blindness and had an inner strength, something I could hold on to during my darkest hours of anxiety and despair. I knew I needed Jesus: His touch, His presence, His hand to help me. And I reached out to Him. He was by my side through every hour of crisis.

I listened to Ethel Waters as she sang, "His eye is on the sparrow and I know He cares for me," with tears streaming down my cheeks. My heart cried out, "Oh God, if You care that much for little sparrows — You care for them, You clothe them and feed them — surely, You'll care for me. God, I'm Your child." I had walked with Him and had talked with Him and I needed Him more desperately than I had ever needed Him before.

I listened to Jack Holcomb sing, "Until then, my heart will go on singing. . .until the day, God calls me home." But I couldn't sing. I had lost my song. I felt so convicted about not singing praises to my Lord. I prayed, "Oh Lord, give me a song upon my lips so that I can sing with joy once again." God answered that prayer as I meditated on the words, "More about Jesus would I know, more of His grace to others show" and "It is no secret what God can do." All of the old songs of the faith were very precious to me. I can never express how deeply my soul was touched.

One day, after about three weeks of blindness, I began to realize that "life is God's gift to us. What we do with our life is our gift back to the Lord" (author unknown). Life would be what I would make it to be, no more, no less. It was up to me. I wanted to be able to give a life back to Jesus that was worthy of His death on Calvary. It was hard to venture out. But slowly I began to pick up those broken pieces.

Depressed and frustrated with myself and my life, I felt a desperate need to find a secret closet — a place to pray. One evening, following the mid-week prayer service at church, my heart was particularly heavy. With a family of nine people at home, I had no place where I could pray without feeling I was being heard by my brothers and sisters.

After the prayer service was dismissed, we started home. My heart was aching. I had to go somewhere to pray — anywhere but home. I worked up the courage to ask my Dad if he would drive me to the home of our associate pastor, Garland Cofield, which he did. Arriving at the Cofields, I asked Pastor Cofield if he would mind my spending the night in his study. It was located on the lower level of the house and was very private. I was embarrassed to ask this favor, but I knew I had to.

Pastor and Mrs. Cofield graciously opened their home to me that night. A pillow and blanket were laid out on the living room couch for me to use if and when I felt ready for it. I prayed and cried most of the night. Blind and shattered, I felt my heart was breaking. Surely God had a plan and a purpose for my life. If I could only know God's will. What was I to do? I prayed and wept throughout the night.

It is the ministry of the Holy Spirit to make intercession for the saints. Paul assured us of this in his letter to the Romans. He said, "Likewise the Spirit also helpeth our infirmities: for we know not what we should pray for as we ought: but the

Spirit itself (Himself) maketh intercession for us with groanings which cannot be uttered. And he that searcheth the hearts knoweth what is in the mind of the Spirit, because he maketh intercession for the saints according to the will of God" (Romans 8:26-27/KJ). The Holy Spirit prays through our human bodies, the temples in which He dwells. That night, He showed Himself to me as my intercessor.

God works when we recognize that we are at the end of our human resources. If we are truly trusting in the Lord, we do not need to be afraid. God released His power over me and gave me a free spirit of victory, joy, and peace over my inner struggle of fear and anxiety.

I was God's child, He had delivered me from hell unto salvation and would surely care for my needs now. He could be trusted to work out this devastating problem. So I went to bed on the sofa about 4:00 a.m. with such peace in my heart, knowing things would be all right!

I felt the impression that the Lord wanted me to attend Tennessee Temple Bible College. I knew this was part of His plan for me. I didn't know all that was in His plan, but I had a deep, settled peace of knowing that He was leading me there. I would study with the use of a tape recorder and take my tests orally.

Later that morning at the breakfast table, Pastor Cofield asked me, "Did you get any word from the Lord?" I didn't know how to answer. I did not fully understand what that night had meant to me or how to explain the peace which I felt. Truly it was God's peace and there were no words to explain it. I had gained strength and direction for my life through that night of prayer. It was a turning point for me.

In Genesis, we are told of an incident in the life of Jacob: "Jacob rose up in the middle of the night. Being alone, there wrestled a man with him till the breaking of the day. And when he saw that he prevailed not against him, he touched the hollow of his thigh,and the hollow of Jacob's thigh was out of joint as he wrestled with him. And he said, 'Let me go, for the day breaketh.' And Jacob said, 'I will not let thee go, except thou bless me'" (Genesis 32:26/KJ).

Chapter Two

The Necessity of Total Commitment

WE ALL HAVE MANY BOUTS with the devil. He always tries to make us think we are far less than what God tells us we are. In overcoming the "accuser of the brethren," we need to remember what Paul says: "Who dares accuse us whom God has chosen for His own? Will God? No! He is the one who has forgiven us and given us right standing with Himself. Who then will condemn us? Will Christ? NO! For He is the one who died for us and came back to life again for us and is sitting at the place of highest honor next to God, pleading for us there in heaven" (Romans 8:33-34). It is God who is in control. It is He who rules and challenges Satan. We just need to recognize that all of our sufficiency is in Jesus Christ our Lord.

When we fail to apply the blood of Christ to the devices of Satan, we become depressed, discouraged and sometimes feel that the walk of righteousness and true holiness cannot be lived or attained. In ourselves we can't, but we place our confidence solidly in Christ. God asks that we come before Him in total helplessness.

Remember, in the blood of the cross we find forgiveness and deliverance. Many Christians do not realize that they have already been delivered from the old life. Paul told the Corinthians, "When someone becomes a Christian he becomes a brand new person inside. He is not the same any more. A new life has begun!" (II Corinthians 5:17). Some say they just cannot give up their sin. If we cannot, then God is a liar. "He will show you how to escape temptation's power so that you can bear up patiently against it" (I Corinthians 10:13b). The fact is, God has already given us the power to turn from sin. When we accept the fact that He has done this for us, then we can gain release from the sin that besets us.

Sin Hinders Prayer

Listen to David as he writes with joy and excitement: "Come and hear, all of you who reverence the Lord, and I will tell you what he did for me: For I cried to him for help, with praises ready on my tongue. He would not have listened if I had not confessed my sins. But he listened! He heard my prayer! He paid attention to it! Blessed be God who didn't turn away when I was praying, and didn't refuse me his kindness and love" (Psalm 66:16-20). David was conscious of the need to confess sin before he brought his requests into the presence of the Lord. Harbored sin in the life hinders the Lord from hearing our prayers.

It is normal for Christians, born of the Spirit of God, to covet spiritual development and to forsake worldliness and sin. The Christian lays aside his self life. It is abnormal for him not to do this because he is now born of the Holy Spirit and cannot enjoy the things of the world anymore.

Christians experience a full salvation — salvation unto eternal life as well as daily salvation from sin. This is true due to our position in Christ. The Holy Spirit has released us from the power of the old nature. Our "desires" and "want-to's" have changed. Things once loved are no longer desired.

God's people must develop a deep sense of those things that displease the Lord. Each one of us is personally responsible for sin in our lives. Sin must be exposed, denounced, confessed and forsaken. We must hate sin, recognizing that it offends a Holy God.

Personal faith in Christ demands holy living. Paul wrote to Titus, "For the free gift of eternal salvation is now being offered to everyone; And along with this gift comes the realization that God wants us to turn from godless living and sinful pleasures and to live good, God-fearing lives day after day" (Titus 2:11-12). It is our responsibility to progress in holiness and in a disciplined life. We are not to seek ways to satisfy our evil, fleshly desires.

Paul said, "So, dear brothers, you have no obligations whatever to your old sinful nature to do what it begs you to do. For if you keep on following it you are lost and will perish, but if through the power of the Holy Spirit you crush it and its evil deeds, you shall live. For all who are led by the Spirit of God are sons of God" (Romans 8:12-14).

Watchman Nee said, "Just asking for the Spirit to take complete authority over our soul is a wrong assumption, for unless 'we' deliver to death our

natural life, its power and self-will; unless we
wholly desire in our mind and will to obey and rely
wholly upon the Holy Spirit, we will not see Him
actually performing. We must be ready to have
His life so fill our Spirit that the soul life is
immobilized. The Lord uses His Word to separate
Soul and Spirit. Be willing to obey every 'word' as
God has commanded."

We are not to live in bondage to the flesh but are
to actively cooperate with God as He works in our
lives. Neither the devil nor Christ can do anything
in our lives without our consent. Our strength to
overcome sin and wrong comes through the
resurrection power of Jesus Christ within us. If
God is going to deliver us, then we must allow
Him to do it. This is accomplished as the deeds of
the body are put to death by the Holy Spirit and by
the act of our will. It is futile to try to reform or to
change. Rather, we must declare ourselves dead
to sin. As Paul wrote, "So look upon your old sin
nature as dead and unresponsive to sin, and
instead be alive to God, alert to Him, through
Jesus Christ our Lord" (Romans 6:11). As
Christians, we need to be sold out to Jesus Christ
with a heart that yearns to live a holy life. Solomon
wisely said, "Winking at sin leads to sorrow; bold
reproof leads to peace" (Proverbs 10:10).

Jesus said, "If you insist on saving your life, you
will lose it. Only those who throw away their lives
for my sake and for the sake of the Good News will
ever know what it means to really live" (Mark
8:35). Paul wrote to the Colossians, "And this is
the secret: that Christ in your hearts is your only
hope of glory" (Colossians 1:27).

Jesus did not resist the devil in the wilderness in His own strength. He received the enablement of the Holy Spirit. We, too, must depend on the enablement of the Holy Spirit to resist Satan's temptations. We need to learn to focus our eyes on Jesus rather than on our sins. The writer to the Hebrews wrote, "Looking unto Jesus the author and finisher of our faith" (Hebrews 12:2a/KJ). Solomon said, "For as a man thinketh in his heart, so is he" (Proverbs 23:7/KJ). We need to give all of our failures and weaknesses to Him in prayer.

Andrew Murray wrote: "The Spirit of obedience, the sacrifice of self, bestows the value, the infinite value of the cross. Here God reveals to us the secret of the power of that blood. The blood could not have been shed, apart from a similar sacrifice of self on the cross. So it cannot be received apart from a similar sacrifice of self. The blood is a living, spiritual heavenly power. It will cause the soul that is entirely surrendered to it to see and know by experience that there is no entrance into the full life of God except by the self-sacrifice of the cross.

"How free and unhindered is our access to God and how truly His blessings may flow toward us. There is now nothing, absolutely nothing to hinder the fulness of the love and power of God from coming to us and working in us, except only our unbelief and slowness of heart.

"Let us meditate on the power which the blood has exercised in heaven until our unbelief is conquered and our right to these heavenly powers, by faith, fills our lives with joy. The power of the cross is in the blood."

John wrote, "Loving God means doing what He tells us to do, and really, that isn't hard at all; For every child of God can obey Him, defeating sin and evil pleasures by trusting Christ to help him" (I John 5:3). Our attitude must be: I have the armor of God, I am able to stand against the strategies and wiles of the devil (Ephesians 6:11). I will drive out the enemy from the field of battle (James 4:7).

In Psalms we read, "Happy are those who are strong in the Lord, who want above all else to follow your steps" (Psalm 84:5). The devil has no power, no authority over me as long as I walk in the fear of God, as long as I (the branch) stay hooked to the vine. He can't get me unless I walk in sin and give him room to enter my life.

To those who walk in righteous living before God He promises, "It will be well with thee" (Isaiah 3:10/KJ). All your needs will be supplied (Philippians 4:19). You will have "abundant provision" (Psalm 132:15) and "soul satisfaction" (Proverbs 13:25). Also, you are promised "prolonged days of life" (Deuteronomy 5:23 and also Proverbs 10:27). You will "come to the grave in full life" (Job 5:26). God says, "He will heal all our diseases" (Psalm 103:7-8). His Word is health (medicine) to all our flesh (Proverbs 4:22). In Luke 9:56 we read, "the Son of Man is not come to destroy man's life but to save them."

God attracts us to Himself like a magnet. Our spirits are drawn to Him by His Spirit. Through the prophet Jeremiah God said, "You will find me when you seek me, if you look for me in earnest" (Jeremiah 29:13). Unless we are willing to confess our sin and forsake it, we will never have power with God in prayer. We either turn from our sins and receive God's blessings, or we continue in our sins, satisfying our worldly appetites and receive God's judgments through troubles on every hand.

Sin Robs Us of Blessings

Thomas Eliff in his book, *The Power of Prayer,* says, "Somehow we Christians feel that sin can be isolated in an otherwise religious life and God will wink at it." I believe that many Christians fail to deal with their sins and have little desire to turn from the habitual sin in their lives. One of the major reasons the work of the Holy Spirit is not more effective today is because there is so much unconfessed sin. Isaiah said, "But the trouble is that your sins have cut you off from God. Because of sin he has turned his face away from you and will not listen anymore" (Isaiah 59:2). In other words, He will simply tune you out. Christians with unconfessed sin in their lives are among the most miserable people on earth.

God said, "O that there were such an heart in them, that they would fear me. . ." (Deuteronomy 5:29a/KJ). People claim to be Christian believers but do not have hearts to obey God. We obey the promptings of God because we have His Spirit within us wooing us to do so.

We live in a day when sin is not called what it is: SIN! God requires holiness in the lives of believers, nothing less. The Psalmist David prayed, "And keep me from deliberate wrongs; help me to stop doing them. Only then can I be free of guilt and innocent of some great crime" (Psalm 19:13). David asked God not to allow any

sin at all to creep into his life, or, if it did, not to
allow it to have a hold on him. He desired to be
"confessed-up."

We read in Haggai, "Consider your ways, you
have sown much, but you bring in little. You
drink, but you are not filled. You clothe
yourselves, but there is none to warm. You earn
wages, only to put them in bags with holes. Think
it over says the Lord of hosts, consider how you
have acted and what has happened as a result"
(Haggai 1:5-7).

How can we have power to overcome sin? The
answer can be found in the book of John where we
read, "You are already clean because of the word
which I have spoken to you" (John 15:3/NAS). It is
the Word which cleanses. It is the Word which
has the power to convict. The Psalmist wrote, "Thy
word have I hid in my heart that I might not sin
against thee" (Psalm 119:11/KJ). We must get into
the Word. "Resist the devil and he will flee from
you" (James 4:7/KJ). "Take the sword of the Spirit,
which is the Word of God, and with the shield of
faith quench the fiery darts of the wicked"
(Ephesians 6:16-17/KJ). Begin to use God's Word
as a power in your life. Cultivate trust in it. Let it
control your soul. Problems come when we fail to
recognize the power we have in the blood. We
must activate that power. Pray in faith. The Word
will not work unless we believe it and act upon it.

Confession Brings Forgiveness

When we ask for forgiveness, we receive it because
our sins are covered by the blood of Jesus Christ.
The blood of the cross deals with deliverance from

the sins of our past, present, and future. God tells us that "we are made to be the righteousness of God in Christ Jesus" (II Corinthians 5:21). We are totally righteous before God. It's a gift from God. That's our position. What I am talking about is our standing in "holiness of life," not our "righteous position." We cannot be more righteous than we are already in Him, but we certainly can become holier. Because we are righteous, we can live a life of holiness through the power that God gives us. It takes commitment. It does not happen automatically.

As a born-again child of God, I knew I was positionally right with the Lord. But in my spirit I knew daily confession had to be made in order that nothing would stand in the way of my fellowship with God. John wrote to believers, "But if we confess our sins to Him, He can be depended on to forgive us and to cleanse us from every wrong. [And it is perfectly proper for God to do this for us because Christ died to wash away our sins]" (I John 1:9). God says, "Your sins have separated between you and your God that I will not hear your prayers" (Isaiah 59:2). In other words, if we have sin in our lives and we refuse to repent, confess and turn from it, our prayers are never heard before the throne of God.

When we sin, we have an immediate awakening of our spirit by the Holy Spirit that we have sinned against Almighty God. Our fellowship is broken and we are vulnerable to Satan. He will snatch conviction from our hearts because he wants us to forget about confessing our sin.

There are two principles we need to understand when we do sin. First, positionally we are still in

God's family. Because we are under the blood, Satan cannot alter our position in Christ. However, we are automatically out from under the place of God's blessings and protection. Second, when we ask for forgiveness, we will receive it. The precious blood of Jesus Christ redeems us from all sin and from the penalty of death which would otherwise be upon us. There is a sin unto death for a Christian who habitually sins (I John 5:16). The writer to the Hebrews says, "And having a high priest over the house of God; Let us draw near with a true heart in full assurance of faith, having our hearts sprinkled from an evil conscience. . ." (Hebrews 10:21-22a/KJ).

Many Christians do not realize that daily cleansing of their consciences is available to them and absolutely necessary.

We cannot get right with God by penance, by trying to be holy, by reading the Bible more, or by more faithful church attendance. Granted, these things can help to bring us closer to God. True fellowship with God is gained only by confessing sin and putting it under the blood of Christ. A clear conscience is never attained by our own works but by the work of Jesus Christ on the cross of Calvary. All a person needs to do is to accept what Christ did for him, confess his sins and turn from them.

In this life, we will never understand fully the power in the blood of Jesus Christ. However, one thing we do know, the blood of Jesus satisfies God as the payment for our sin. Because of that fact, it is possible that you and I can walk in a continued overwhelming realization of Jesus Christ Himself and His presence with us at all times, being fully accepted in the beloved.

Chapter Three
The Necessity of Discipline

WE ARE TO ENDURE the hardship of discipline which the Lord brings to us. Solomon said, "You are a poor specimen if you can't stand the pressure of adversity" (Proverbs 24:10). Discipline is of such importance that this Proverb is quoted in Hebrews which reads, "And you have forgotten that word of encouragement that addresses you as sons: My son, do not make light of the Lord's discipline, and do not lose heart when he rebukes you, because the Lord disciplines those he loves, and he punishes everyone he accepts as a son" (Hebrews 12:5-6/NIV).

God treats His children exactly as we are to treat our children. If we do not discipline them, we really do not love them. Likewise, if God did not discipline us for the wrong which we do, He would not love us. The motivation for discipline is love.

Paul wrote to the Corinthian church of the hardships he had endured. (Read II Corinthians 11:16-33.) Paul knew what it was to suffer. He experienced exhaustion — was tired, weary and fatigued. He was bitten by a snake, was beaten, and was often put into prison. Paul knew what it was to suffer. Christians in the early church lived in a world very hostile to the gospel. They accepted the suffering they experienced daily with joy, because they knew God would bring them out of all of it. Paul didn't rejoice in the trial itself, but in the God who was able to deliver him. We don't rejoice in the bad things Satan brings upon us. We rejoice in God who will give us the victory. He will deliver us. Remember Jesus said, ". . .In the world ye shall have tribulation: but be of good cheer; I have overcome the world" (John 16:33b/KJ). Praise God, we can be fully persuaded that God's will is to deliver us, and He will do it!

Growing Nearer to God Through Difficulties

God uses tribulation and trials to bring us closer to Himself. They help us to experience the deeper work of the cross by producing the character of God in us.

The Psalmist David says, "Many are the afflictions of the righteous; but the Lord delivereth him of them all" (Psalm 34:19/KJ). He also writes, "You have let me sink down deep in desperate problems, but you will bring me back to life again, up from the depths of the earth" (Psalm 71:20). And again, "For he has not despised my cries of deep despair; he has not turned and walked away. When I cried to him, he heard and came" (Psalm 22:24).

The prophet Hosea says, "Come, let us return to the Lord; it is he who has torn us — he will heal us. He has wounded — he will bind us up" (Hosea 6:1). In Lamentations Jeremiah declares, "For the

Lord will not abandon him forever. Although God gives him grief, yet he will show compassion, too, according to the greatness of his lovingkindness. For he does not enjoy afflicting men and causing sorrow" (Lamentations 4:31-33).

Remember the Holy Spirit makes intercession for us. When "we don't even know what we should pray for, nor how to pray as we should; but the Holy Spirit prays for us with such feeling that it cannot be expressed in words" (Romans 8:26). And in the same way, by faith, the Holy Spirit helps us with our problems and delivers us from them. But too often we come before the Lord with a spirit of intimidation. We need to ask His forgiveness for our sins and then come before Him as He sees us — forgiven and accepted in the Beloved. When we are forgiven and complete in Him, we are given the right to come boldly before His throne. In Hebrews we are instructed, "So let us come boldly to the very throne of God and stay there to receive His mercy and to find grace to help us in our times of need" (Hebrews 4:16).

Stop praying for the same thing over and over. Begin to believe God and start praising Him for the answer. It will not be long before answers to your prayers become a reality. The Psalmist says, "Whoso offereth praise glorifieth me. To him that ordereth his conversation aright will I show the salvation of God" (Psalm 50:23/KJ).

God wants us to take Him at His Word. Sometimes we think our problems are either too big or too small for God and that we shouldn't bother Him with them. When finances aren't available and nothing is going our way, we neglect to turn these needs over to the Lord and trust Him to supply the need. The Apostle Paul says, "I pray that you will begin to understand how incredibly great His power is to help those who believe Him. It is that same mighty power that raised Christ from the dead and seated Him in the place of honor at God's right hand in heaven" (Ephesians 1:19-20).

There is nothing God cannot do for us. He has promised to supply all our needs according to His will. Charles Allen wrote: "God is our source of supply and His blessings are not limited by the human resources that are available." We must never forget that He will give us everything we need to carry out His plan for our lives upon earth.

Power Through Difficulties

Pressure in the Christian's life can produce power. It has been said, "More pressure, more power." But many times, without the feel of pressure, our prayers are powerless. The greater the pressure and the more closely we come to being crushed, melted down and remolded, the more earnestly we will seek the face of God in prayer. In Hebrews we read, "And even though Jesus was God's Son, He had to learn from His experience in the wilderness fighting off Satan's temptations, what it was like to obey, when obeying meant suffering. "It was after He had proven Himself perfect in this experience that Jesus became the Giver of eternal salvation to all those who obey Him" (Hebrews 5:8-9). As Jesus Christ, God's Son learned obedience by means of the things He suffered, so do we. As He was perfected through His sufferings to become the author of eternal salvation, so are we being perfected by the pressure points in our lives.

Our prayers will become more fervent and with a sense of deeper urgency as we experience and endure the pressure. Our prayers will no doubt be powerless and remain that way until we are confronted with pressure of some kind.

Paul told the Christians at Corinth, "We are hard pressed on every side, yet not crushed; we are perplexed, but not in despair; persecuted, but not forsaken; struck down, but not destroyed — always carrying about in the body the dying of the Lord Jesus, that the life of Jesus also may be manifested in our body" (II Corinthians 4:8-10/NKJV.

When our Christian lives take on pressures like those described by Paul, we have the opportunity to experience the power of prayer. Because of the pressures, we can come boldly and expectantly into God's presence in prayer, knowing that He will answer. He will deliver us from every trial.

Whatever God speaks to your heart when you are reading His Word, learn to rest upon that Word, for it is the sure foundation for your faith. Don't be discouraged because you don't feel His power. Don't let how you feel hinder your faith. Accept God's Word by faith apart from your feelings.

We need to be strong-willed when Satan attacks. We do that by keeping our mind stayed on the Word God has given us. "Thou wilt keep him in perfect peace whose mind is stayed on thee" (Isaiah 26:3/KJ). To have perfect peace in the midst of our storms, we rest our faith on God's promise to us.

Some people think all their problems come from God and therefore they do not resist Satan's attacks. Somehow they think "all things come from God, therefore, I must accept this as God's will." God says, "resist the devil and he will flee from you" (James 4:7b/KJ). They do not understand God's teachings. He says, "My people are destroyed for lack of knowledge" (Hosea 4:6/KJ). Satan is reigning over them (their circumstances) because they do not know what it means to take authority over the devil and gain deliverance from the clutches of Satan.

A strong Christian is one who has learned how to stand on God's promises until the devil has to back off. He is steadfast, immovable and stubborn while standing on the Word. It takes real discipline, determination and diligence to live by God's Word. It's difficult to rejoice when all is going wrong. But if you are standing firmly on God's Word, fully expecting God to intervene, His Word will not return void.

We must learn to praise God in all things. We are not asked to praise Him for the problem, but to praise Him for the answer. Praise Him that He is in control and because "greater is He that is in you than he that is in the world" (I John 4:4/KJ). Satan is a defeated foe when you come against him with the Word and you don't back off in doubt and fear. "Perfect love casteth out fear" (I John 4:18b/KJ).

Correct Misplaced Blame

Don't blame God for all the pressures in your life. We bring many of them upon ourselves and God has nothing to do with them. Satan causes much of it.

You may be frustrated with people on the job. Don't let them ruin your day, your peace, your joy and rob you of victory. Give your frustrations to Jesus. Perhaps you are filled with fear. Recognize that fear is of Satan and not of God. Cast it out. Set your mind on the power of God which works within you. Jealousy, too, is of Satan. It is a wicked thing, and has no reality in it at all. Remember jealousy led ultimately to Saul's suicide.

Financial pressures may plague you. Stop charging. Why pay more for an item than it is worth through unnecessary interest charges? Why throw away the money you have or perhaps the money you do not have? The piling up of bills month by month causes marriage problems which result in misunderstandings, divorces and emotional breakdowns. Perhaps a secret sin has you weighed down in misery. Mental institutions are filled with people who are ridden with guilt over some secret sin. Bring it out into the open and confess it before it destroys you.

Maybe you have become so low that you go about unshaven and with uncombed hair, not caring for yourself as you once did. You have become too lazy to take the effort to be well groomed. This is often a sign of poor mental health, a personality disorder. It shows a poor self-image and a lack of self-respect. Maybe you think you should have things better in life than you actually do. You blame others and your circumstances for your condition. However, you have actually allowed yourself to become the way you are. You have set your own standard (or lack of it). Cleanliness and neatness bring respect and prosperity. Take a good hard look at yourself. People see you as you are. Your outward appearance speaks for you. It is up to you to do something about it.

The person of the world has a reason to fall apart, but not God's child. The Kingdom which is in you is righteousness, peace and joy. You are to receive God's joy for living and keep it burning within you — on the job, in the home, everywhere you go. In the world, "Men's hearts are failing them for fear" (Luke 21:26/KJ). Isaiah said, "Thou wilt keep him in perfect peace whose mind is stayed on thee, because he trusteth in thee" (Isaiah 26:3/KJ). If you do not place your trust in God, you will fail. The Psalmist said, "They that meditate on God's Word shall be like a tree planted by the rivers of water, that bringeth forth fruit in his season, his leaf also shall not wither, and whatsoever he doeth shall prosper" (Psalm 1:3/KJ). Take stock of yourself. Train your mind to think in God's way, and then walk in that peace of mind.

Never look at your circumstances. Instead see God's miracle provision by focusing your eye of faith on the Scripture — that Word of God that covers your need. Do not doubt God's revealed Word to you. Continue to quote the Scriptures— Scriptures that cover your need or situation—to yourself and to God in prayer. Remember faith is believing that you have received based on what God has spoken. You must be able to accept God's Word as truth, as fact, or you will not be able to walk in faith.

Paul writes, "We can rejoice, too, when we run into problems and trials for we know that they are good for us — they help us learn to be patient. And patience develops strength of character in us and helps us trust God more each time we use it until finally our hope and faith are strong and steady" (Romans 5:3-4). The greater our testing, the greater will be our opportunity to experience His power.

James instructs us, "Dear brothers, is your life full of difficulties and temptations? Then be happy. For when the way is rough, your patience has a chance to grow. So let it grow, and don't try to squirm out of your problems. For when your patience is finally in full bloom, then you will be ready for anything, strong in character, full and complete" (James 1:2-4). Going through pressure problems makes us stronger in the Lord and brings great rewards. We all have difficulty in receiving answers to prayer at times. If you are praying in accordance to God's revealed will and are getting a delay, remain fervent in your prayer. Persevere with determination until the answer comes. With your entire being, let your prayer to God rise in intensity and claim God's Word. The devil may be blocking your prayer answer from getting through, or the delay may be an instrument used by God on your behalf to bring you to higher attainment in the pursuit of prayer. Learn to see the pressures of life in this light.

I like a chorus Bill and Gloria Gaither have written which says:

> Hold on my child, joy comes in the morning,
>   Weeping only lasts for the night.
> Hold on my child, joy comes in the morning,
> The darkest hour means dawn is just in sight.

This simply means that when things look their worst, if we are trusting God, our trials and pressures can bring us to a deeper trust in our Lord Jesus Christ, if we will let them. Joy comes when we've learned what it means to resist the devil and do not allow him to take from us those things that God has promised us in His Word. We grow in strength as we use the authority that has been delegated to us as believers to overcome every testing by the power and use of the name of Jesus. There is power in the blood. Cover your pressures with His blood.

When we develop the maturity of a good understanding as to why we have pressures and trials, we will then be better equipped to become the prayer warriors God wants us to be.

Ask the Lord for the spirit of faith. Allow it to fully possess you. When you pray, all doubt will vanish as you pour out your heart to God for the needs of your life. Know that Jesus has baptized you with His Holy Spirit. React by faith and trust Him to work in you the joy of power in the Holy Spirit. Yield your heart continually to God in order to receive answers from Him. Prayer in the Holy Spirit will become a power in your life. Live by faith in Jesus Christ, not in your own faith. With this faith in Jesus, He will supply the blessings you need.

Many who claim to be God's children are ignorant of the precious treasures of wealth God has for them. They are weary, weak and feeble because they have not become mighty in prayer. However, as they yield to the Holy Spirit to take control of their entire lives, allowing the nature of Christ to replace their old sinful natures, the power of prayer in Jesus' Name that's available to them will be released in and through them.

Truly prayer is our greatest power upon earth.

Faith Is Built Through Adversity

There are times when we must welcome adversities because they will build our faith. In Romans we read, "Not only so, but we also rejoice in our sufferings, because we know that suffering produces perseverance; perseverance, character; and character, hope. And hope does not disappoint us, because God has poured out his love into our hearts by the Holy Spirit, whom he has given us" (Romans 5:3-5/NIV).

James says, "Consider it pure joy, my brothers, whenever you face trials of many kinds, because you know that the testing of your faith develops perseverance. Perseverance must finish its work so that you may be mature and complete, not lacking anything" (James 1:2-4/NIV). We need to let faith persevere until we receive the desired blessing.

God does not promise us a life of ease. Rather, He tells us that suffering and trials will come. Our attitude in handling them will determine the development and growth of our faith. We may not understand what God is doing in our lives, but we must be obedient to Him regardless of the circumstances.

The Genesis story of the life of Joseph perfectly illustrates the exercise of faith in the midst of trials. Joseph's brothers were jealous of him for the special relationship he had with their father, Jacob. So they sold him to the Egyptians as a slave and told their father he was dead.

In Egypt, after having been given a position of authority, he was thrown into prison for being falsely accused by Potiphar's wife. Later, he was released from prison and returned to his place of authority, second in command to the Pharoah. Years later, at the time of a great famine, his brothers came to Egypt to buy grain. Ultimately he was restored to his family and cared for their needs. What Joseph's brothers meant for evil, God meant for good.

Through all of the trials in his life, Joseph never doubted God. Instead Joseph exercised faith. God was in control of his life. His trials were brought about by Satan working through others. If Joseph were alive today, he would probably say that God used his trials and turned them around for his blessing and good. In naming his sons, it is written, "And Joseph named the first-born Manasseh, 'For,' he said, 'God has made me forget all my trouble and all my father's household' And he named the second Ephraim, 'For,' he said, 'God has made me fruitful in the land of my affliction'" (Genesis 41:51-52/NAS). Through much heartache, spiritual character and strength were developed. God used Joseph's trials for His glory and blessed him tremendously later in life.

This principle, written by Paul to the church at Rome, is practiced today by all growing Christians. Paul says, "And we know that in all things God works for the good of those who love him, who have been called according to his purpose" (Romans 8:28/NIV). God will use everything and anything that comes into our lives for our good and His glory as we love Him and obey what He tells us to do. Look at Paul's summary, ". . .in all these things we are more than conquerors through him who loved us. For I am convinced that neither death nor life, neither angels nor demons, neither the present nor the future, nor any powers, neither height nor depth, nor anything else in all creation, will be able to separate us from the love of God that is in Christ Jesus our Lord " (Romans 8:37-39/NIV). What incredible promises these are.

Paul tells us in Ephesians, "God will give you spiritual wisdom and insight to know more of Him and that you might receive that inner illumination of the Spirit which will make you realize how great is the hope to which He's calling you. I rejoice in the magnificence of the inheritance promised to Christians and the tremendous power that is available to us who believe in God" (Ephesians 1:16-23/Phillips).

Resurrection Power

In Philippians we are challenged to "experience'" the power of His resurrection. Paul says, "Now I have given up everything else — I have found it to be the only way to really know Christ and to experience the mighty power that brought Him back to life again, and to find out what it means to suffer and to die with Him" (Philippians 3:10). Many Christians are unaware of the power available in His resurrection — power to die to our sinful desires, power to defeat Satan and his wiles. We are to lay hold on the power that's in the blood.

In Paul's letter to the Romans he wrote that we never will be able to die to our fleshly desires on our own. He said, "But there is something else deep within me, in my lower nature, that is at war with my mind and wins the fight and makes me a slave to the sin that is still within me. In my mind I want to be God's willing servant but instead I find myself still enslaved to sin.

"So you see how it is: my new life tells me to do right, but the old nature that is still inside me loves to sin. Oh, what a terrible predicament I'm in! Who will free me from my slavery to this deadly lower nature?" He continues by saying, "Thank God! It has been done by Jesus Christ our Lord. He has set me free" (Romans 7:23-25). There's our victory! Thank God!

Only God has the power to put our sinful desires to death. He redeemed us from the power of sin. Therefore, it has no more power over the believer as he acknowledges his position in Christ. We can conquer sin only by recognizing our crucifixion with Christ and by appropriating our resurrection to new life in Him. See yourself in the light of God's Word. You have living in you all the power and authority of God Himself.

Satan can do nothing to us without first checking with God. He has no power over the believer except for what we allow him to have and what God permits for our spiritual growth. Though we may accept God's grace for forgiveness, at the same time we may neglect God's grace for deliverance. Christ did not come to redeem the flesh but to destroy it. This is worked out in the life of the believer as he dies to self (the flesh).

God has provided a complete salvation which is to be enjoyed in complete triumph. It is our responsibility to die to self and live unto God according to the finished work of Jesus Christ on the cross.

Andrew Murray wrote: "We are to lay hold on the blood and make its power active in our soul. Where the blood is honored, appropriated and believed in as the power of our full redemption; therein is the way opened for the fulness of the Spirit's blessings on your individual lives.

"We think of the blood as an event that happened 2000 years ago. Do you see the blood as present and real today? Do you know what the blood can do? Honor the blood and its power to overcome every hindrance. When Jesus died, His blood had power to conquer sin and death. So that Jesus was brought again from the dead by the blood of the everlasting covenant. When I rely on the blood, Jesus makes its power glorious in me. The blood is all-powerful in its effects. We often limit the continuance of it's activity to a period of our own active cooperation with it. As long as your faith is actively engaged with it, the blood will manifest its power to you. Commit yourself to the sanctifying power of the blood."

God says, "Whatsoever touches the altar shall be holy" (Exodus 29:37). In the Old Testament we learn that the blood had the power to cleanse and sanctify anything that the people laid upon the altar. This remains true for us today. What I lay on the altar is sanctified and made holy. I must believe that what I have given is accepted by God. Only then can the blood exercise its power.

Positions Do Not Insure Spirituality

Just having a position in a church does not make a person spiritual and pleasing in the sight of God. Spiritual persons are those who have an ongoing, day-by-day walk with the Lord in the power of the Holy Spirit.

When we know what to do to maintain a growing relationship with the Lord and avoid it, we are sinning. James says, "Remember, too, that knowing what is right to do and then not doing it is sin" (James 4:17).

As Christians share their testimonies, teach, preach or sing in the power of their own strength, God may bless what they say, but there is not the power behind it. When I rely on my own strength, ability and charisma, I am relying on the flesh and not upon God. At times like this, I am a carnal Christian and not doing the will of God.

Experiencing the power of the Holy Spirit is not something which can be taught. You cannot teach another person how to experience the power of the Holy Spirit. It must be encountered, one on one, by going the way of the cross.

We must pray that God will help us to talk according to the Spirit and to do nothing without first seeking His guidance. In Proverbs Solomon wrote, "Trust the Lord completely; don't ever trust yourself. In everything you do, put God first, and he will direct you and crown your efforts with success" (Proverbs 3:5-6). There is such a difference when we minister in the Spirit and not in the power of our own flesh. God wants us to be His instrument. Learn to flow with Him. It's the only way the Spirit can operate through us. He will not force His power upon us. We must open ourselves up to Him and allow Him to work His power through us. We can gain much power by praising God that we are redeemed and that we have victory over the works of the devil through the promises He gives us in His Word.

The times we fall down in failure and defeat can become times of victory. These experiences should remind us of what the Apostle Paul said: "For I can do everything God asks me to with the help of Christ who gives me the strength and power" (Philippians 4:13). When we rely on His strength, defeat can be turned into victory. Failure and defeat should ignite a chain reaction in our hearts to confess sin and to renew our fellowship with God.

The Lord Is Our Source for Victory

I remember, when a potentially discouraging defeat by Satan actually turned out to be a great victory. God's ready answer to prayer caused me to praise Him.

I have driven thousands of miles in the past years going to speaking engagements. I have always dreaded having a flat tire on an Interstate highway. On Interstate 40, between Memphis and Jackson, Tennessee, I was having such a great time with the Lord, praising Him in word and song, when a tire blew out. I told the Lord I feared some of the weirdos who travel the highways. I asked Him to send someone to help me whom I could trust.

I got out of the car, opened the trunk, and found a spare tire and a little steel jack which was foreign to me. I had no idea as to where to place the jack under the car nor how to use it.

While I was removing the tire out of the trunk, a car pulled over and a very handsome, well-dressed man got out. I immediately thanked the Lord and told Him He had done a good job — this man looked like a child of His. As the man approached, I told him how much I appreciated his stopping to help me. He seemed to radiate Christ-likeness. He then proceeded to take the flat tire off and put the spare on. He struggled in getting the nuts off the wheel. I realized there was no way I could have done that by myself.

As he was finishing, I opened the door of the car and asked him which he liked better, books or tapes. I wanted to give him a copy of my book, *These Blind Eyes Now See*, or a cassette tape of my testimony. He replied, "I like both." It was then that he told me that he was a Baptist minister. I said, "Praise the Lord!" I told him that my husband was also a Baptist minister. I was so thankful and praised God for sending one of His ministers to help me. He meets our every need if we ask Him.

Moving with God is the functioning of the Holy Spirit within you. He is omnipresent — He is everywhere. "His promises and gifts are to all that are afar off, even to those whom God shall call"

(Acts 2:38-39). Seek after God's gifts. Earnestly covet to know God. Be determined to operate in God's power and you will experience His victory on the battlefront of life.

Chapter Four
What God Taught Me About Prayer

PRAYER IS THE OPENING of our heart's door to Jesus. It is a precious time spent in intimate, joyous fellowship with the Lord. The more we pray the easier and more meaningful it becomes.

At the start it may seems quite hard and require rigid discipline over our mind and will, but after practicing what we know to be right, it will become a habit, a natural time of communing with Him.

Prayer is really an attitude of our spirit. When we go to the Lord in prayer, we must have the "faith to believe" that He will hear and answer our prayers. This faith will come only through hearing God's Word and being obedient to it.

No matter how difficult our situation may be, God's Word remains truthful. Someone has said, "Not to believe in God's Word is one of the greatest sins of our world today." Never, never say "I don't have faith." Stir up the measure of faith God has given you. Learn how to make it come alive. It's yours and you already have it. Now begin to use it.

Release your faith in the Words God has spoken. Know that if God said it, it is true and it will work for you.

You must know that you are sure that that which you are asking God for is His will. You know and are sure because you have His Word on it. Now hold to that Word and don't give up. Do not base your faith on your circumstances or how you feel. Faith is not dependent on how you feel, neither is it just hoping God will answer, it's knowing He will. Then faith is not just sitting doing nothing. God says "faith without works is dead" (James 2:26b/KJ). Faith is a powerful force within us that comes alive when we study the Word. Then based on that Word, with the act of our will, by faith we chase out all doubt, fear, anxiety and frustration. If you are struggling with faith, having a long sad countenance saying, "I am trying," that is not faith either. Faith is just there. It is solid. It is based on God's Word which does not return void (Isaiah 55:11).

Meditation Adjusts Our Attitudes

Meditation on the Word of God is necessary if our attitude toward sin is to be adjusted. The Psalmist teaches us, "But they delight in doing everything God wants them to, and day and night are always meditating on his laws and thinking about ways to follow him more closely" (Psalm 1:2). This verse places great importance on time spent in meditating on the Word of God. God has given us so much in the Bible He wants us to know. And the only way we will learn these things which He has for us is through meditation.

When we read and study the Bible and find a tidbit which really means something special to us, we should write it down and memorize it. We should meditate on it throughout the day. It will be amazing what will be learned each time it is brought to mind. We should take that tidbit from God's Word and give it back to God in prayer. Mull it over in our mind. Get it into our spirit.

After it is memorized, we should share what has been learned with someone else. Mid-morning, call someone on the phone or visit with a fellow Christian and tell them what has been learned. Each time it is shared, more will be learned. At lunch time, give that which was learned back to God in prayer. Then, try to find someone else to share it with during the afternoon. At night pray it back to God once again and then think how much was learned from that one piece of Scripture that day. Look forward to tomorrow with anticipation at the new lesson God will teach.

Another way to meditate is to "pray-read" the Scripture. It will be surprising how praying back the Scriptures helps in understanding them better and increases the effectiveness of one's prayer life.

Let's use Psalm 1, taking each thought and praying about it in relationship to yourself personally. It says, "Blessed is the man that walketh not in the counsel of the ungodly . . ." (Psalm 1:1/KJ). When seeking counsel, ask Him to guide you to a dedicated Christian who will give you wise advice and guidance. We are not to seek counsel from those who do not know God. Pray, "Lord, help me not to seek counsel from unbelievers."

Then the Psalmist says, "Blessed is the man that
. . . standeth not in the way of sinners" (Psalm
1:1/KJ). Pray, "Lord, may I not be a stumbling
block to anyone coming to know Christ." A
stumbling block is something which causes
another person to doubt whether life in Christ is
the only way because of what is seen in your
lifestyle.

He goes on to say, "Blessed are those that . . .
sitteth not in the seat of the scornful" (Psalm
1:1/KJ). Ask, "Lord, keep me from having a
critical attitude or a judgmental spirit, or from
sowing discord among the brethren or even with
members of my own family."

We are also encouraged, ". . . in His law doth he
meditate day and night" (Psalm 1:2/KJ). Valuable,
profitable time should be spent during the day and
the night recalling those things God has taught us
from His Word. Meditation seals His Word within
our minds and helps us to remember what He has
taught us, particularly when temptation arises.
So pray, "Lord, help me to meditate in Your Word
today!"

Verse three of Psalm 1 is most precious. It
assures remarkable promises to the person who
will walk a holy life. "And he shall be like a tree
planted by the rivers of water, that bringeth forth
his fruit in his season; his leaf also shall not
wither; and whatsoever he doeth shall prosper"
(KJ). What a beautiful promise! God promises
prosperity in whatever is done to the man who will
live a life separated unto Him. And what an
incredible promise to claim. We can pray, "Lord, I
claim this promise today. If I meditate on Your
Word, my leaf shall not wither and whatever I do

today shall prosper. Thank You, Jesus!" When we "pray-read" and meditate in this manner much will be learned from the Word of God, and God will honor this time spent with Him.

Activate the Will

Coming to the Lord with believing faith is an act of our will. In Hebrews we read, "You can never please God without faith, without depending on Him. Anyone who wants to come to God must believe that there is a God and that He rewards those who sincerely look for Him" (Hebrews 11:6). The reward for seeking the face of God is offered to us by God Himself. Joshua wrote, "Not one word which God has spoken shall fail" (Joshua 2:4).

In I Thessalonians we are admonished to "Always keep on praying" (I Thessalonians 5:17). This means we are to be diligent in prayer and in a constant attitude of prayer day and night. We can pray for the people whom we see while walking along a sidewalk, or people we work with on the job. It could be the first time anyone has ever prayed for them.

E. M. Bounds wrote that prayer is "a discipline to maintain." He said, "I have so fixed the habit of prayer in my mind, that I never raise a glass of water to my lips without asking God's blessing. I never seal a letter without putting God's Word under the seal. I never take a letter from the post box without setting my thoughts heavenward. I never leave my lecture room without praying for the cadets who go out and for those who come in."

Now that is what it means to "always keep on praying." We must learn to make prayer a vital part of every moment of our lives. We should be so accustomed to praying at all times that it is just as natural as breathing. Just be sure you do not pray the same request over and over using vain repetition.

You may ask, "What do you mean by that?" We are to make our request known unto God. Then after we have prayed and found rest in our hearts over the situation or request, God's peace permeates our heart and mind. Then, we have confidence and are fully persuaded that God has heard and answered our request.

However, if we come to God making that same request in the same format of prayer, we will use vain repetition. In order not to do that, we must change the form of prayer regarding the particular request. John wrote, "And this is the confidence that we have in Him that if we ask anything according to His will, he heareth us; and if we know He hears us, whatsoever we ask we know that we have the petitions that we desired of him" (I John 5:14-15/KJ).

As this "confidence" takes hold, we then pray a prayer of praise and thanksgiving over that request. We may say, "Lord, I thank You that You have heard my prayer for my son. Thank you for the protection of Your angels over him as he is out in the world. May no evil befall him. Thank You that the Holy Spirit is working in his life, convicting him of his wrong way. May Your Holy Spirit bring him to salvation through the blood of Jesus. Because he is in Your hands, I can sleep in peace. Praise You, Lord. I know I've received Your answer."

righteousness? Are you thirsty for God? Only He can quench that burning desire within you. Seek after God with all your heart, soul and mind. Be willing to pay the price.

Take the old hymns of the faith and dwell upon their words. Meditate on them prayerfully and allow them to be the rejoicing of your heart.

Strengthened by the Holy Spirit

Paul prayed for the Christians at Ephesus, "That out of His glorious, unlimited resources He will give you the mighty inner strengthening of His Holy Spirit. And I pray that Christ will be more and more at home in your hearts, living within you as you trust in Him. May your roots go down deep into the soil of God's marvelous love; And may you be able to feel and understand, as all God's children should, how long, how wide, how deep, and how high His love really is; and to experience this love for yourselves, though it is so great that you will never see the end of it or fully know or understand it.

"And so at last you will be filled up with God Himself. Now glory be to God who by His mighty power at work within us is able to do far more than we would ever dare to ask or even dream of — infinitely beyond our highest prayers, desires, thoughts, or hopes. May He be given glory forever and ever through endless ages because of His master plan of salvation for the church through Jesus Christ" (Ephesians 3:16-21).

In order to make the fact of our crucifixion with Christ effective in our lives, we must in faith surrender our "old self" to God. Paul wrote, "Well then, shall we keep on sinning so that God can keep on showing us more and more kindness and forgiveness? Of course not! Should we keep on sinning when we don't have to? For sin's power over us was broken when we became Christians and were baptized to become a part of Jesus Christ; through His death the power of your sinful nature was shattered.

"Your old sin-loving nature was buried with Him by baptism when He died, and when God the Father, with glorious power, brought Him back to life again, you were given His wonderful new life to enjoy. For you have become a part of Him, and so you died with Him, so to speak, when He died; and now you share His new life, and shall rise as He did.

"Your old evil desires were nailed to the cross with Him; that part of you that loves to sin was crushed and fatally wounded, so that your sin-loving body is no longer under sin's control, no longer needs to be a slave to sin; For when you are deadened to sin you are freed from all its allure and its power over you. And since your old sin-loving nature 'died' with Christ, we know that you will share His new life" (Romans 6:1-8).

We will then think His thoughts, take on His desires, and strive to do those things which are pleasing in His sight. It is possible to live such a dedicated life. As we seek to live a holy life, Jesus Christ will make Himself real to us day by day. As we ask Him for His help, He will renew His character within us.

Paul continued, "So look upon your old sin nature as dead and unresponsive to sin, and instead be alive to God, alert to Him, through

Jesus Christ our Lord. Do not let sin control your puny body any longer; do not give in to its sinful desires. Do not let any part of your bodies become tools of wickedness, to be used for sinning; but give yourselves completely to God — every part of you — for you are back from death and you want to be tools in the hands of God, to be used for His good purposes" (Romans 6:11-13).

We are to declare our old desires as dead with Christ and claim our new desires in the resurrection of Christ. We are to rely upon, roll over upon or trust God by faith to produce His life through our flesh. Remember we cannot crucify self; we are to declare it dead. We do not need to give in any longer to bad attitudes, selfishness and pride, the old sins of the flesh or to the temptations of the devil.

We read in Romans, "So there is now no condemnation awaiting those who belong to Christ Jesus. For the power of the life-giving Spirit — and this power is mine through Christ Jesus — has freed me from the vicious circle of sin and death. We aren't saved from sin's grasp by knowing the commandments of God, because we can't and don't keep them, but God put into effect a different plan to save us. He sent His own Son in a human body like ours except that ours are sinful — and destroyed sin's control over us by giving Himself as a sacrifice for our sins.

"So now we can obey God's laws if we follow after the Holy Spirit and no longer obey the old evil nature within us. Those who let themselves be controlled by their lower natures live only to please themselves, but those who follow after the Holy Spirit find themselves doing those things that please God" (Romans 8:1-5). And this leads to life and peace.

As the children of God, sometimes our hearts are so uncertain and we feel God is so far away from us. Our confidence and assurance sometimes fluctuates. We must learn to develop a spirit of complete trust in Him that is not based on our feelings.

God has provided a oneness in Christ for us. Our trust in God by faith is based upon our position in Christ. We can come boldly to the throne of Grace, anytime and anywhere. All who have been elected, chosen, born again, cleansed by the blood of Christ and resurrected in Him, have the right and authority to come into the presence of Almighty God fearlessly and with boldness. Always remember a clean conscience is necessary for great faith. Ours is a high and holy calling of God in His Son, Jesus Christ. However, if your heart condemns you, then it is likely that you have sinned. On the other hand, the devil sometimes accuses God's children unjustly.

When we feel depressed, have a lack of assurance and confidence toward God, Satan has been effective in cutting off our communication with our heavenly Father. He sends these feelings to us to hinder our prayers and make them ineffective. We must guard against his attacks. He takes away our desire to pray, makes us feel unworthy of God's provisions and causes us not to trust God to answer. Satan is working against us all of the time. He makes us feel restless, unhappy and out of sorts. He robs us of our joy and peace. Paul had to resist Satan and thus the evil spirit left him. Satan is overcome by the blood of the

Lamb. Permit the Holy Spirit to take control of your life! Don't be hesitant or defeated when you don't feel God's power. It's not how you feel that counts — just believe God and accept it by faith.

We should not hesitate to believe God when His will has already been predetermined through His Word. Rather than spending precious time in prayer about something that has already been determined through His Word, we should merely remember what the Word says and thank God for its power. When we are abiding in His will and confessing our sins daily, we do not have to worry about being in God's will. We are already there. Praise God!

Chapter Seven
God Seeks Intercessors

GOD HAS ALWAYS sought intercessors but few are willing to make the sacrifice. Isaiah said, "And he saw that there was no man, and wondered that there was no intercessor . . ." (Isaiah 59:16/KJ). Later Isaiah wrote, "O Jerusalem, I have set intercessors on your walls who shall cry to God all day and all night for the fulfillment of his promises" (Isaiah 62:6).

Norman Grubb, in his book, *Intercession*, clearly states a difference between a prayer warrior and an intercessor. He writes, "A prayer warrior can pray for a thing to be done without necessarily being willing for the answer to come through himself; and he is not even bound to continue in the prayer until it is answered. An intercessor, on the other hand, is responsible to gain the objective and he can never be free till he has gained it. He will go to any length for the prayer to be answered through himself." An intercessor takes the needs of others upon himself as his very own.

Andrew Murray said, "Prayer is the key that opens the door for God Himself to do His work in us and through us." The prophet Ezekiel wrote, "I looked in vain for anyone who would build again the wall of righteousness that guards the land, who could stand in the gap and defend you from my just attacks, but I found not one" (Ezekiel 22:30).

It is the desire of God that we develop such a deep concern for others that we become intercessors in prayer for them. Most Christians pray regularly for their families and others close to them, but very few ever reach the level of seeking to become an intercessor for the needs of people and ministries, perhaps less familiar to them. When God lays a burden or special prayer request upon us, we must see this as a special privilege He has bestowed upon us. But, along with this privilege comes the responsibility to intercede for the needs of that request until it is met. You will be compelled to pray and meet that need through God by prayer as though you are the answer.

If God burdens us to intercede, rather than just becoming a prayer partner, we must intensely pray for that request with diligence and determination. We must talk not only with God about the request, but we must also check regularly as to the progress being made in that for which we've committed ourselves to pray and put works behind our prayers. Remember, ". . .faith without works is dead" (James 2:20b/KJ). We take on the burden as though it were our very own, agonizing in prayer, if need be until relief comes.

As we continue to intercede for that need, and keep abreast of the progress being made in God's answer, God will bless us in ways beyond our imagination. The burden to intercede must be placed upon our hearts by God or we will not have the unction to pray it through. Making intercession is not a joyful experience, neither is it a time of worship toward our Lord. It's a time of pain and agony. Overcoming a difficulty through prayer brings us eternal blessings and makes importunate prayer our highest privilege.

We must not lose our courage to persevere with God in prayer while going through a period of what appears to be a refusal. Hold your steadfast assurance of obtaining the desired blessing. Be occupied with God's power and know, "This is my God and He will bless me." Refuse to give up until it is manifested.

Paul wrote to the Galatians, "Share each other's troubles and problems, and so obey our Lord's command" (Galatians 6:2). I never consider it a chore to enter into prayer fellowship with another person. A great time of rejoicing comes when a specific request, which both of us had diligently prayed for, is miraculously answered.

God tells us to bear one another's burdens. But let me warn you not to carry another's problems. Bear them in prayer but do not carry them. You'll become so weighed down you won't know how to handle it. Let Jesus carry your troubles and theirs also.

I am often asked to speak to different groups on subjects such as "The Fear of God," "The Power of the Resurrection," and "Prayer." One evening while having dinner with a pastor and his wife before a meeting, the pastor said, "I sense in my spirit that you are an intercessor." He then poured out his heart to me about their two sons. I agreed to join with them in prayer and kept in touch with

them for over two years. God answered with
incredible results. Jesus said, "For where two or
three gather together because they are Mine, I
will be right there among them" (Matthew 18:20).

Some requests are of such nature that they
become as heavy and as weighty a burden upon
my heart as they are upon the heart of the
individual who shared the request with me. I
struggle alongside them for God's answer. There
is great power in the prayer of an intercessor on
behalf of someone else.

James says, ". . . The earnest prayer of a
righteous man has great power and wonderful
results" (James 5:16b). Never allow the world and
its responsibilities to take place over your prayer
time. Guard it. Treasure it. Give yourself to it. It
is not possible to go into a prayer mood of
intercession quickly. It takes heart preparation:
time spent with God in deep abandonment and a
personal devotion to the Lord before one can move
into the depths of prayer.

I feel there are many times that the Lord wants
to do great and mighty things in and through our
lives, but He withholds His blessings because we
Christians fail in our ministry of intercession.

A good example of this principle is to be found in
an Old Testament account about the nation Israel.
God wanted to "increase the house of Israel," but
did not do so, simply because His people had not
talked with Him (prayed) about it. Finally, when
the Israelites did inquire (pray) of Him as to why
He had not increased them in number, the Lord
told them it was because they had not (prayed)
requested it of Him. In other words, before God

carried out what He had already planned to do, the people had to ask Him to do so in prayer.

To intercede for a particular matter that God has burdened us to pray for and experience the gaining of the promised possession may not always be easy, even though God wills it.

In Isaiah we read, "O Jerusalem, I have set intercessors on your walls who shall cry to God all day and all night for the fulfillment of his promises. Take no rest, all you who pray, and give God no rest until he establishes Jerusalem and makes her respected and admired throughout the earth" (Isaiah 62:6-7).

In other words, the Lord is saying that He willed to do this for Israel but He would not proceed. He waited for His people to come to Him, expressing their desire and agreeing with Him in the matter of "making Jerusalem respected and admired throughout the earth." They were instructed to pray day and night "taking no rest" or "giving God no rest" until the answer came. They gave themselves to persevering prayer over something that was already pre-ordained of God. Yet He did not answer until they had interceded in prayer.

Intercession As A Way of Life

Intercessory prayer is not a one-time prayer. The Holy Spirit draws us by His power and enlarges our heart for the work of intercession. Even though it is His will and He draws us, we can expect difficulties. These difficulties are sometimes necessary, but will result in great spiritual attainment. We must refuse to accept "no" for an answer when we know we are praying

according to God's will. We need to exercise faith
in the power of prayer and to persevere with
courage in the face of the road-blocks.

When we persevere, we will see how weak we
are and how little we long to have time with God.
It is a heart-searching process to see our
weakness, sin and failure. However, as we yield to
God's Spirit, fellowship with God becomes so
much sweeter with every trial.

God does not always choose to answer our
request immediately, even when it is His will to do
so. If He did, we would not take the time to search
our hearts and draw closer to our Savior. First He
needs to cleanse our hearts from all that
displeases Him: the flesh, self, and the world.
Through trials we are taught to delight ourselves
in Him, the Giver, rather than in the gift. It is so
important that we learn to delight ourselves in the
Giver. To thank Him and to Praise Him.

Many of God's intercessors struggled much in
prayer. Abraham prayed five times for God to
spare Sodom. "Finally, Abraham said, 'Oh, let not
the Lord be angry; I will speak but this once more!
Suppose only ten are found in Sodom who love
God, would You spare the city?' And God said,
'Then, for the sake of the ten, I won't destroy it'"
(Genesis 18:32).

Also in Genesis we read of Jacob as he wrestled
in prayer with an angel: "And when the Man saw
that he couldn't win the match, He struck Jacob's
hip, and knocked it out of joint at the socket. Then
the Man said, 'Let me go, for it is dawn.' But
Jacob panted, 'I will not let you go until you bless
me'" (Genesis 32:25-26). John Wesley wrote, "God
will do nothing except as people ask Him."

Because God loves us, He does not always satisfy our every desire quickly. He tells us in II Chronicles, ". . . keep up the good work and don't get discouraged, for you will be rewarded" (II Chronicles 15:7). We are always to believe in the Giver. God will answer in His time. Remember the words of James, ". . .the earnest prayer of a righteous man has great power and wonderful results" (James 5:16b). Persevering prayer is needful if we are ever to obtain God's richest blessings. Do not give up when it seems that God will not answer.

In Hebrews we read, "Do not let this happy trust in the Lord die away, no matter what happens. Remember your reward! You need to keep on patiently doing God's will if you want Him to do for you all that He has promised" (Hebrews 10:35-36). Paul instructs us, "So my dear brothers, since future victory is sure, be strong and steady, always abounding in the Lord's work, for you know that nothing you do for the Lord is ever wasted as it would be if there were no resurrection" (I Corinthians 15:58). Proverbs says, "My gifts are better than the purest gold or sterling silver! My paths are those of justice and right. Those who love and follow me are indeed wealthy. I fill their treasuries" (Proverbs 8:19-21).

Who knows how many blessings we have forfeited because of our failure to intercede to God for the spiritual and material needs of our Christian family, both individuals and ministries? Perhaps the Lord is waiting for us to share in these blessings through agonizing in intercessory prayer. We read in Joel, "Fear not, be glad or rejoice for the Lord will do great things" (Joel 2:21).

Releasing God's Power

Intercessory prayer releases God's power through our lives. When we attend church we know God wants men and women to be saved and for Christians to confess sin. However, God may not bring people to Himself for salvation or confession if we fail to pray, asking Him to have His will in their lives. Every church needs those who will become intercessors for the needs of the congregation. Maybe God is waiting for you to begin such a ministry, even if it is by yourself.

We must keep in mind that we cannot put God into a box and manipulate Him into doing as we have decided. When we decide that God is going to do a certain thing in a particular way, He may well choose another way, simply to prove to us that He is God. It is not our job to dictate to God how He should answer a particular request. Our responsibility is to pray. His is to answer as He sees fit.

It is of utmost importance that we develop the habit of praying about every little detail of our lives. Paul wrote to the Philippians, "Don't worry about anything; instead, pray about everything; tell God your needs and don't forget to thank Him for His answers. If you do this you will experience God's peace, which is far more wonderful than the human mind can understand. His peace will keep your thoughts and your hearts quiet and at rest as you trust in Christ Jesus" (Philippians 4:6-7). What beautiful verses. What a powerful promise. Pray about everything and know His peace.

I take these verses literally. I do try to pray about every part of my life. For example: When I go to a speaking engagement, I ask the Lord for a safe trip and to give me a comfortable motel room so I can be well rested and can do my best in what He has for me to do the next day. When I get up in the morning, I pray on the way to the restaurant that God will provide me a good, nourishing meal. I ask God to make the fellowship I have with friends edifying, enjoyable and encouraging. At mealtimes I pray for the waitress or waiter who will be serving me, that I might be a witness for Christ to them. I pray for God's protection as we drive our cars — Acie, as he drives to the church and on his calls; Sharon, as she drives to the University each day — that God's angels will continually protect them. I really do try to pray about as many details as I can — little things, big things, whatever comes to mind. The more details I pray about, the less there is that goes wrong.

Upon rising in the morning, before or after breakfast, spend at least a half hour with the Lord in prayer and in His Word. Try to do the same in the afternoon. Feast upon the prayer promises in the Word and pray over them. Lift your heart to God in faith throughout the day as you are occupied with a multiplicity of tasks. Seek God in prayer moment by moment for His guidance. Be sensitive to the movement of the Spirit in your innermost being, then seek to follow His leading. Honor God's most holy presence by giving the Spirit complete authority over your soul, and you will have learned how to walk in the Spirit. It's a

real discipline to maintain. When the end of the
day comes your heart will be at peace. You will
have enjoyed sweet fellowship with the Lord all
day. Before going to sleep you may only need to
say, "Good night, Lord Jesus. I love You!"

This kind of praying will keep us from
backsliding. Prayer before meals and at bedtime
will serve only to help us maintain a distant walk
with God wherein we will experience little power
with God. Continual prayer to God allows us to
reach to higher levels of God-consciousness with
more growth, more strength, and more of His
leadership. It enables us to experience God's
power and to make His blessings real in our lives.
When we are drawn to prayer by God's Spirit, we
must learn to receive His answer by faith. Jesus
said, "Didn't I tell you that you would see a
wonderful miracle from God if you believe?" (John
11:40).

When our daughter, Sharon, was very young,
she was afraid to be alone in the darkness at
bedtime. I had taught her that Jesus was with her
and that she need not be afraid. One night she
said to me, "Momma, Momma, I see the angels in
my room. They're everywhere. There are so many
they have to fold their wings so they can all get in."
After that, every time she became afraid she
would say, "God's angels have come in to watch
over me." What beautiful, child-like faith. It is this
kind of faith, knowing that God hears and will
answer, that gives power to our prayers.

We need to allow the Holy Spirit to take over and
possess every area of our lives — our thoughts,
our actions — all that we do. We must die to our
fleshly need to always think our own thoughts. We

must discipline our minds to think on the majesty of God, of His power, and His faithfulness.

The Holy Spirit within you needs to flow out to fill your soul and your body to edify others. God's Spirit requires an outlet. Our Lord Jesus Christ used the power of the Holy Spirit, as did John the Baptist, Matthew, Mark, Luke, John, Peter, Paul, and a host of other New Testament believers who are our examples to follow.

The Holy Spirit is already living in every Christian. Set your spirit free so there can be an outpouring of the Holy Spirit through your life, an outflowing of joy and power. Let the Holy Spirit motivate you, soul and body. Let your joyful eagerness surface. You and I must let this happen. Allow God's Spirit to flow through you. When people see God's joy, love and peace in you, then they will want it too.

Jesus said, "But you are to be perfect, even as your Father in heaven is perfect" (Matthew 5:48). The only way we can walk blameless before God is to live in uninterrupted fellowship with the Father and in His presence at all times. This is accomplished as a life of prayer is interwoven into our activities of the day. This very special walk with the Lord will require much discipline in the beginning — until it becomes a natural lifestyle.

Dr. Mary Stewart Relfe said, "Prayer is the most powerful force on earth." Oh, that we might know the reality of the words of Paul, "Now we can come fearlessly right into God's presence, assured of His glad welcome when we come with Christ and trust in Him. . . . When I think of the wisdom and scope of His plan I fall down on my knees and

pray to the Father of all the great family of God —
some of them already in heaven and some down
here on earth — that out of His glorious,
unlimited resources He will give you the mighty
inner strengthening of His Holy Spirit.

"And I pray that Christ will be more and more at
home in your hearts, living within you as you
trust in Him. May your roots go down deep into
the soil of God's marvelous love; And may you be
able to feel and understand, as all God's children
should, how long, how wide, how deep, and how
high His love really is; and to experience this love
for yourselves, though it is so great that you will
never see the end of it or fully know or understand
it. And so at last you will be filled up with God
Himself.

"Now glory be to God who by His mighty power at
work within us is able to do far more than we
would ever dare to ask or even dream of —
infinitely beyond our highest prayers, desires,
thoughts, or hopes" (Ephesians 3:12, 14-20).

When praying, we should not ask in
generalizations. We need to be specific about each
request. Rather than pray for all sick people, pray
for the sick folks we know, by name. Rather than
pray for all missionaries, pray for the
missionaries we know, by name. Rather than
thank God for all His blessings, thank Him for
each blessing, by name. Like the words of the old
hymn:

Count your blessings, Name them one by one;
Count your blessings, See what God hath done.

God will at times bring the burden of a particular person or ministry to mind. When this happens, stop what you are doing and pray for that situation right then. Being an intercessor is costly. But we as Christians must choose to obey God as we "Share each other's troubles and problems, and so obey our Lord's command" (Galatians 6:2). This is not an option. It is a command. Let's pay the price. We'll be glad when we do, for it pays big dividends.

My personal prayer is: "God, enable me to pray in the power of the Holy Spirit, according to Your will. Manifest Yourself powerful through my life and prayers. When I pray, it is my desire to know that I am praying according to Your will, and therefore, I will know that You have heard my prayer and I can expect to receive from You what I have requested." I make this my definite request to God daily. In my heart I thank Him in advance for it because His Spirit has borne witness with my spirit in the matter. I simply trust the words of Jesus when He said, "Listen to Me! You can pray for anything, and if you believe, you have it; it's yours" (Mark 11:24).

This reminds me of a time when I had tucked away $200 so well I couldn't find it. Days passed and I had looked everywhere. At that time, $200 was like $2,000 to us, and therefore, I was very anxious to find it. I prayed, "Lord, please help me to find it." One day, God gave me a particular Scripture verse: ". . . Keep on looking and you will keep on finding. . ." (Luke 11:9b). I based my faith on that verse. With my heart lifted in praise and thanksgiving to God, I began looking again, and found it that very day. To be sure, God hears, He answers, and He guides. He is faithful to His Word.

When the Holy Spirit bears witness with your spirit that something is God's will and you have prayed accordingly, doubt, struggle and disbelief will vanish. If fear should overtake you, remain on your knees and find strength in His promises. Your desire to pray constantly and consistently will overwhelm your spirit. Remember His words, "If you believe, you have it." Be faithful in intercessory prayer and the Spirit will do His work through you as His vessel. Be assured that He has heard you and just claim the answer by faith.

The Holy Spirit is in you to give you grace and strength to dare to hold out your confidence in Him. He is working in you to bring about the will of the Father. Christ is our life. When we intercede, we become one with Christ in the work that He is willing and ready to accomplish. Humble yourself before God so that by prayer, His power can be brought down to earth. Note the words of Luke: "And if even sinful persons like yourselves give children what they need, don't you realize that your heavenly Father will do at least as much, and give the Holy Spirit to those who ask for Him?" (Luke 11:13). Our source is our heavenly Father.

Remember the words of Paul to the Ephesian Christians, "I pray that you will begin to understand how incredibly great His power is to help those who believe Him. It is that same mighty power that raised Christ from the dead and seated Him in the place of honor at God's right hand in heaven" (Ephesians 1:19-20). This power is available to believers in the here and now

— today! We will not need it when we get to heaven. John assures us, "For whatsoever is born of God overcometh the world, and this is the victory that overcometh the world, even our faith" (I John 5:4/KJ).

Prayer is powerful. It is through prayer that His power is made available to us. Prayer unleashes the power of the Holy Spirit through us to our world. Reach out and touch God in prayer until He pours out His Holy Spirit upon you. When your life is clean, you can come before His throne of grace with holy boldness.

The desire to have "power with God" needs to be the number one priority of our Christian lives. If you desire to have God's power, seek it and pray for it continuously. Let that one desire absorb your every thought and prayer more than anything else. The Psalmist David wrote, "Be delighted with the Lord. Then he will give you all your heart's desires" (Psalm 37:4).

In an earlier Psalm David said, "The one thing I want from God, the thing I seek most of all, is the privilege of meditating in his Temple. living in his presence every day of my life, delighting in his incomparable perfections and glory" (Psalm 27:4). Do not allow other desires to crowd out your main objective. The quality of time you spend in prayer will determine the power with God that you will have in your life, work and ministry.

The Apostles prayed, "And now, O Lord, hear their threats, and grant to Your servants great boldness in their preaching. After this prayer, the building where they were meeting shook and they were all filled with the Holy Spirit and boldly preached God's message" (Acts 4:29, 31). The anointed Word of God is powerful. It breaks every yoke of bondage.

It is God's will that all Christians be filled with His power. Jesus said, "For the Scriptures declare that rivers of living water shall flow from the inmost being of anyone who believes in Me" (John 7:38). John wrote, "But dearly loved friends, if our consciences are clear, we can come to the Lord with perfect assurance and trust, And get whatever we ask for because we are obeying Him and doing the things that please Him" (I John 3:21-22). To be an intercessor, filled and controlled by the power of the Holy Spirit is our highest privilege. God waits for those who will pay the price of sacrifice and commitment. Paul said, ". . . we are more than conquerors through him that loved us" (Romans 8:37b).

When we pray, the power of God is poured out through our spirits and bodies. The Holy Spirit works through people's bodies and the only bodies He has are yours and mine. God desires to bestow His blessings and power upon us to do His work. The Holy Spirit, given to Christians first at Pentecost, comes to dwell in every born-again child of God at salvation.

Following salvation, each individual Christian needs to allow the Holy Spirit to work through his or her life. He desires to control our activities, filling and refilling us with His power as needed. However, God only gives His power to clean vessels; those who are pure in heart and living the holy life that God expects of each of those who have been washed in the blood of Calvary.

Prayer can reach as far as we can believe God. Oh, that we would not allow anything else in our lives to rob us of the time that we so desperately need to spend at the feet of Jesus. Nothing is more important than staying on our knees in prayer until God's purpose is accomplished. We must be willing to do away with all excuses for not spending time in prayer. We are admonished in the Scripture, ". . . Love the Lord your God with all your heart, soul, and mind" (Matthew 22:37).

Paul writes, "And God is able to make all grace abound toward you; that ye, always having all sufficiency in all things, may abound to every good work" (II Corinthians 9:8/KJ). If we are unwilling to pay the price and make the necessary sacrifices to be an intercessor, God will not bless us and His power will not flow out through us to others.

As we pray, we truly must trust God to answer. If we do not learn to trust Him and take Him at His Word, we will never become successful intercessors, or for that matter, Christians who are pleasing to Him. The writer to the Hebrews says, "And so, dear brothers, now we may walk right into the very Holy of Holies where God is, because of the blood of Jesus. . . . Let us go right in, to God Himself, with true hearts fully trusting Him to receive us" (Hebrews 10:19, 22a). With sin confessed, we can come before God in prayer with great boldness and assurance. It is not because we deserve it, but because God has given us this privilege.

Believing God Brings Boldness

After Pentecost, Peter and John were taken before the elders and chief priests. When they were released, being warned not to speak in the name of

Jesus, they assembled in prayer with the church. Then we read, "And when they had prayed, the place was shaken where they were assembled together; and they were all filled with the Holy Ghost, and they spake the word of God with boldness" (Acts 4:31/KJ). This group of early church Christians, when threatened by the religious leaders, sought the Lord in prayer. God answered by filling them with the Holy Ghost and by giving them great boldness to speak in the name of Christ. The question is: Where is our boldness and power today?

We have been blessed with a tremendous heritage and a great inheritance. Paul wrote the Galatians, "And now that we are Christ's we are the true descendants of Abraham, and all of God's promises to him belong to us" (Galatians 3:29). Jesus said, "Ye shall know the truth and the truth shall set you free" (John 8:32/KJ). These spiritual blessings are already ours.

When Jesus died, we died. When Jesus arose, we arose. We too have been crucified and resurrected – past tense. Paul said, "I have been crucified with Christ: and I myself no longer live, but Christ lives in me. And the real life I now have within this body is a result of my trusting in the Son of God, who loved me and gave Himself for me" (Galatians 2:20).

Where then is our boldness to ask God to bestow upon us all that He wills and to believe that He will do so? The Bible is filled with wonderful descriptions of all that we are and have in Christ. We do not even have to pray for those blessings because they are already ours. How then do we appropriate them? By faith. By simply believing

that God means what He says to us in His Word
and by simply acting upon it. When we keep
asking God for those things that we already
possess, we are walking in unbelief and God will
not and cannot honor unbelief. We need to learn to
accept God's promises by faith. Faith is not a
dream-world of hope. It's having a knowledge of
God. It's knowing what God has already provided
for us.

How do we come boldly before God? We come
before God in the righteousness of Jesus Christ.
God does not look upon us as sinners for He
cannot look upon sin. Rather, He looks upon us as
His children through the righteousness of His
Son, Jesus Christ. Paul wrote, "To the praise of
the glory of his grace, wherein he hath made us
accepted in the beloved" (Ephesians 1:6/KJ). Come
to Him boldly without continual self-
condemnation. God wants our coming to Him in
prayer to be the joy of our lives. He desires to
answer our prayers.

Jesus said, "You haven't tried this before, [but
begin now]. Ask, using My name, and you will
receive, and your cup of joy will overflow" (John
16:24). Accept the fact that we already are made
righteous in Christ. In Colossians we read, "For
He has rescued us out of the darkness and gloom
of Satan's kingdom and brought us into the
kingdom of His dear Son, Who bought our freedom
with His blood and forgave us all our sins"
(Colossians 1:13-14).

You still may ask, "But what about the sin
problem?" The old sinful nature — the flesh —
died when Christ died. Reckon it so. Paul
declared, "For you have become a part of Him, and

so you died with Him, so to speak, when He died; and now you share His new life, and shall rise as He did. Your old evil desires were nailed to the cross with Him; that part of you that loves to sin was crushed and fatally wounded, so that your sin-loving body is no longer under sin's control, no longer needs to be a slave to sin;

"For when you are deadened to sin you are freed from all its allure and its power over you. And since your old sin-loving nature 'died' with Christ, we know that you will share His new life" (Romans 6:5-8). We must reckon ourselves dead unto sin and alive unto God. Declare it so! If we go on living to the dictates of our old nature, we lose fellowship with God and His blessings upon our lives. What God says to us through the Word is powerful. Listen to it. Apply it. Believe it and be set free! The moment you surrender to the Lord He empowers you with His Holy Spirit. You don't need to beg, struggle or agonize over your desire to have His infilling and outflowing power. All He asks is our total surrender and that we embrace Him lovingly.

As believers, we must go on to maturity and experience the power of the resurrection of Christ in our daily lives. At salvation we are given life in Christ and also are given deliverance from the power of sin. Recognize the position that is ours in Christ, forsake the grip of sin, declare ourselves dead to all that is worldly, and walk in the power of the resurrection.

Be bold in Christ! We as Christians already have been delivered from Satan's power. As John wrote, "But if we walk in the light, as he is in the light, we have fellowship with one another, and the blood of Jesus Christ his Son cleanseth us from all sin" (I John 1:7/KJ).

Jesus lives in us, and therefore, Satan has no right to take over Jesus' body. We must take authority over the Devil. We can be delivered from any habit or besetting sin. Jesus said, "And those who believe shall use my authority to cast out demons . . ." (Mark 16:17a). This is His promise. Stand on it! We need to take hold of the authority that is ours in Jesus Christ. Let's be bold for Him.

Paul instructs us, "Just as He had always planned to do through Jesus Christ our Lord. Now we can come fearlessly right into God's presence, assured of His glad welcome when we come with Christ and trust in Him" (Ephesians 3:11-12). I really like that part, "assured of His glad welcome when we come with Christ and trust in Him." If we have confidence in something or someone, we already possess the most important ingredient to accomplish a task.

There may be times when we come before God in prayer and we have no confidence because of unconfessed sins. However, after we have made confession, claiming His promise to forgive, we then can have the confidence to come boldly into His presence and to make our requests known unto Him.

Blessed indeed are those who are in a position to draw near to Almighty God and to come to Him in prayer with "boldness and confidence." Paul says, "And the Father who knows all hearts knows, of course, what the Spirit is saying as He pleads for us in harmony with God's own will" (Romans 8:27). What a powerful promise! We can pray according to the will of God even as the Holy Spirit prays for us. When we come to the Lord in this way, with our minds tuned to His mind, we will pray according to His Spirit within us.

Remember, the only time Satan can rest is when the saints are not praying. It is said, "The Devil trembles when he sees the weakest saint on his knees" (author unknown). It just makes good sense that the more we pray, the more power we will be able to exercise over Satan.

Praying in the Spirit

What about praying in our inner spirit? We must be alone in a place where we are closed off from everything and everybody. A place free from all distractions. Jesus teaches us in His Sermon on the Mount, "But when you pray, go away by yourself, all alone, and shut the door behind you and pray to your Father secretly, and your Father, who knows your secrets, will reward you" (Matthew 6:6). We need to close out everything from the outside world. God's Spirit will relate Himself with our spirit as to what to pray. It is this "Spirit connection" that is so important.

The greatest book known to man is the Bible, the written revelation of God. But greater still is Jesus Christ, the living revelation of God. He will reveal Himself to any person who wants Him to do so, whether they can read the Bible or not.

Jesus tells us, ". . .for the Kingdom of God is within you" (Luke 17:21b). Our fullest attention must be given to the deep, innermost part of our being. God, in the person of the Holy Spirit, lives within us and His presence is with us at all times. In Psalms we read, "Stand silent! Know that I am

God! . . ." (Psalm 46:10a). In the quietness of our own hearts we acknowledge who He is and give Him honor as the King of Kings and Lord of Lords. He is the mighty, awesome, powerful God. We come to Him, calling upon His name in prayer and then wait in silence before Him. It is amazing those things He will reveal to us in that silence.

Praying in the Name of Jesus

Another principle we must remember is that we should always pray in the name of Jesus. As children of God, it is our blood-bought privilege to pray in Jesus' name. God longs for His children to recognize and appropriate the power available to them in the name of His Son, Jesus. Things changed in Jesus' life after the Holy Spirit came and took full possession of Him at His baptism. This same power that was given to Jesus has now been designated to all believers. When Jesus ascended, He delegated that power and authority to believers of all ages.

Jesus said, "You can ask Him (the Father) for anything, using My name, and I will do it, for this will bring praise to the Father because of what I, the Son, will do for you. Yes, ask anything, using My name, and I will do it" (John 14:13-14). Since the day of Pentecost when the Holy Spirit came in power upon all those who were met in the upper room, all believers down through the ages have been given this privilege of praying in the name of Jesus. Believers who live by faith and who allow the Holy Spirit to actively live His life through them can avail themselves of that power that is in Christ's name.

Jesus found it necessary and of utmost importance to rise early in order to talk to His Father. Mark writes, "The next morning He was up long before daybreak and went out alone into the wilderness to pray" (Mark 1:35). Before choosing His twelve disciples, Jesus prayed. In Luke we read, "One day soon afterwards He went out into the mountains to pray, and prayed all night" (Luke 6:12). If prayer was this important to Jesus, surely it must be to us as well.

Each time Jesus was to do a mighty work for His Father, He prayed for strength for the task before Him. He sought His Father's face in prayer for His miracle-working power. However, today we often think that we are capable of singing, teaching, or preaching before people without even so much as fifteen minutes spent in prayer to receive the power necessary for the task. God's Son, Jesus, would not have done the work of His Father that carelessly. We must remember that we cannot do the work of God in our own strength. We have no power in ourselves. The power is all in the name of Jesus. However, we must ask for it.

Again Jesus said, "Yes, ask anything, using My name, and I will do it" (John 14:14). The measure of our surrender to Christ determines our power to pray in the name of Jesus. We must have absolute dependence upon the Holy Spirit to take what we do and to use it for His highest glory. To do that, we must pray for the will of God to be accomplished, using the authority given to us in the name of Jesus.

Jesus told His disciples, ". . . I have been given all authority in heaven and earth" (Matthew 28:18b). He gives us the privilege of using that authority. "And those who believe shall use My authority. . ." (Mark 16:17a). It is by faith that we can accept the promise that we have received what we've asked for because God said so. "Abraham by faith called those things that be not as though they were" (Romans 4:17). It wasn't reality yet, but in faith's eye it was done. Verse 21 says that "he was fully persuaded that what God had promised him, God would do."

O. Hallesby, in his book, *Prayer,* wrote: "We must remember that when we come to God, He becomes actively engaged at once in hearing and answering our prayers."

Andrew Murray said, "Christ's one condition for success is to bring us into such dependence on Him that we are not able to do without Him for one single minute. The believer, who in faith allows the Spirit to possess his whole life, can avail himself of all the power of Christ's name." "Abraham who against hope (circumstances), believed in hope that he might be the father of many nations according to that which was spoken" (Romans 4:18). He believed God for what God had spoken. Faith takes God at His Word.

The Spirit will lead us to pray correctly as we are careful not to listen to the voice of our human comprehension. We must abandon ourselves totally to God. When we are not operating in the Spirit, we know it, because when the soul of man (will, mind and emotion) becomes involved, prayer becomes filled with anxiety, frustration and difficulties on every hand. When prayer is of the

Spirit, it is not forced, but is rather very joyous, free and unhindered.

The Spirit of God within us is very powerful. We must keep turning our souls within ourselves to our spirits and rest in the Lord until He reveals Himself to us. Each time our minds wander away from the presence of the Spirit of God, we must draw them back to Him. Satan will try to draw our minds away from God and onto earthly matters. We must not allow the Devil to trouble us or to heap guilt upon us for this struggle within. We must keep on drawing back to His Spirit, keeping the sweet fellowship with God flowing in and through us as we are before Him in prayer.

Chapter Eight
Claiming the Promises of God

PAUL TOLD the Corinthians, "For who hath known the mind of the Lord, that he may instruct him? But we have the mind of Christ" (I Corinthians 2:16/KJ). In writing to the church at Philippi he said, "Let this mind be in you, which was also in Christ Jesus" (Philippians 2:5/KJ). It is important that Christians recognize that the moment we trust Jesus Christ, we receive the mind of Christ. We are His body. He lives in us. We are one with Him.

All of God we will ever have or need is given to us at the moment of salvation. All of the attributes of the Spirit of Christ are ours, including His power. The problem is many Christians are unaware of all they have in Christ. The mind of Christ released in us must be appropriated by us.

When we abide in Christ and stay close to His Word, we have the confidence that we are moving in the Spirit because we have the mind of Christ. The willing cooperation of our mind with His mind go hand in hand. When He opens a door, we are to walk through it. If it is not His door, He will close it.

To have the mind of Christ does not mean that we are to stop thinking. We study and think through each situation with our own minds. Then the Spirit within us will work with our spirit to lead us and move us forward. Oh, to appropriate all that is available to us in Christ Jesus.

We need to develop an awareness of His presence and promptings. The more often He prompts us and we respond affirmatively, the more sensitive we will become to His leading.

Paul wrote, "Always be full of joy in the Lord; I say it again, rejoice!" (Philippians 4:14) and, "Don't worry about anything; instead, pray about everything; tell God your needs and don't forget to thank Him for His answers. If you do this you will experience God's peace, which is far more wonderful than the human mind can understand. His peace will keep your thoughts and your hearts quiet and at rest as you trust in Christ Jesus" (Philippians 3:6-7).

We were created to reciprocate love and to communicate with God in order that He could work His work through us here on earth. His life can only flow through us as we allow Him the freedom to do so. Power in prayer depends upon our trusting God. Paul said, "Let this mind be in you, which was also in Christ Jesus" (Philippians 2:5/KJ).

Jesus prayed continually and He instructs us to "Always keep on praying" (I Thessalonians 5:17). This is not to say that we are to stay on our knees continually but that we are to seek to have a constant flowing out of prayer from our spirits to God. We are to have a spirit of prayerfulness — loving, praising and enjoying God. David said,

". . . so I long for you, O God. I thirst for God, the living God . . . singing with joy, praising the Lord. Why then be downcast? Why be discouraged and sad? Hope in God! I shall yet praise Him again. Yes, I shall again praise him for his help" (Psalm 42:1b, 2a, 4b-5).

In Psalm 37 we read, "Be delighted with the Lord. Then he will give you all your heart's desires. Commit everything you do to the Lord. Trust him to help you do it and he will" (Psalm 37:3-5). God created us for Himself. He wants to live His life in us and accomplish His work through us. He wants us to know that He is working in us and that the power of the Holy Spirit can be demonstrated in our lives as we commit ourselves to Him.

Seeking the Mind of Christ Takes Time

It takes time to know the mind of Christ. We need to enter our prayer chamber and persevere with importunate prayer. Sometimes there is delay because we do not feel Him close when we kneel in prayer. We must wait patiently before Him. We must set our hearts upon God and then He will guide us into all truth. God will give Himself to those who wholeheartedly seek after Him. He will meet us only as we give ourselves to Him. We need to let Jesus occupy our minds and enjoy His presence more than anything else.

When we come to the Lord in prayer, our hearts need to be drawn away from everything around us. The Psalmist wrote, "He is close to all who call on him sincerely. He fulfills the desires of those who reverence and trust him; he hears their cries for help and rescues them. He protects all those who love him, but destroys the wicked" (Psalm 145:18-20). When we truly reverence God and keep His commandments, we will truly know His mind and pray accordingly. His desires will become our desires.

Intuitively, we know when we have found God's will as the Holy Spirit reveals it to us. God will reveal His will to us through a particular passage or verse of Scripture. And when He does, we know it is from Him. From the time we became a child of God by faith, we knew that we had become His child. This knowledge came to us by the enlightenment of the Holy Spirit. We believed and received His promise to us. The same principle holds true in every area of our Christian lives. We simply agree with God and receive His blessings. When we enter into oneness with God, we are given the mind of Christ. Then we can trust our "desires" and "will" to be God's will and desires.

How do you recognize the prompting of the Spirit? It is really so easy. For example: A person sitting in an easy chair at home senses a need to visit someone who is sick or who is a shut-in. That is the Spirit's prompting. Another time a person may feel a need to pray, or perhaps a sermon delivered by a preacher brings conviction of a particular sin and the need to confess it. In practical matters, He may tell you to take a secondary highway off the main route homeward. Later you learn the bridge was out and the Holy Spirit led you to go around. This, too, is His prompting.

Our conscience (innermost intuition) is used by the Holy Spirit to speak to us. When our

conscience tells us to do something, it is probably
the Holy Spirit speaking, and it is imperative that
we follow His leading. I say probably because the
Holy Spirit leads us only in proportion to the time
we spend with the Lord in fellowship and prayer.
Conscience alone can lead us in a wrong
direction. Our conscience must be submitted to the
control of the Holy Spirit, which will be in accord
with the Word of God.

Sin automatically keeps us from experiencing
the power of the mind of Christ in our lives. Fanny
Crosby wrote in her beautiful hymn, *Blessed
Assurance:*

> Blessed Assurance, Jesus is mine,
> O what a foretaste of glory divine.

We can know a "foretaste of glory divine" only as
we strive to live a sin-free life through constant
confession of sin. It is our choice to either give the
control of our lives to the mind of Christ or to the
will of our flesh. God allows each of us the choice
between right and wrong. When we choose to
allow the Spirit to have control by faith through
the Word of God, we will be given the ability to say
"no" to sin. Remember, "Faith cometh by hearing,
and hearing by the Word of God" (Romans
10:17/KJ). Sin can be avoided by our reverence of
God.

Believe God Will Do As He Promises

Be aware that our big sin as believers is not
believing God to do what He says He will do. That
has to grieve the heart of God very deeply. When

sin and disbelief are present in our lives, we cannot claim the promises of God. This is scary. Without the ability to claim the promises of God we are powerless. We must assume the responsibility to deal with sin. This is of maximum importance if we are to keep a right relationship with God. When our relationship with Him is right we can expect Him to keep His promises to us; and He will! God will bring glory to Himself in meeting our needs as we hold a firm faith and trust in Him. Paul said, "And my God shall supply all your need according to his riches in glory by Christ Jesus" (Philippians 4:19/KJ).

As we read and study the Word of God, it will become clear to us that a particular verse is a promise from God which we need to claim. Accept the prompting of His Spirit and claim the promise personally.

A promise from God will spring from the pages of the Bible and lodge itself in our hearts. When God gives us such a promise, we do woll to memorize it and meditate on it during the hours of the day and night. Pray the promise back to God, thanking Him for it, and for what He is doing in your life based on His promise. It will be an anchor and a stronghold in your Christian growth. It will keep you on course and enable doubts and fears to be overcome.

We have the very life of Jesus living in us. Lay hold of this fact and meditate upon it. All that Jesus is is in us. His Holy Spirit in us is Jesus Himself. He has much work to do, but only accomplishes it through us. Paul wrote, "For God is at work within you, helping you want to obey

Him, and then helping you do what He wants"
(Philippians 2:13).

Jesus said, "But an hour is coming, and now is,
when the true worshipers shall worship the
Father in spirit and truth; for such people the
Father seeks to be His worshipers. God is spirit;
and those who worship Him must worship in
spirit and truth" (John 4:23-24/NAS). This is what
God desires of us at all times, not just when we
are in a worship service. As we worship Him in
this manner, He can work through us. As we are
sensitive to His leading and to what He desires to
do in and through us, His Holy Spirit will perform
that which is needful in our lives and through our
lives in helping others. When we pray as we go, it
is prayer breathed in the Spirit. However, when
we fail to pray, the Holy Spirit is "handcuffed."
The power for God to work in and through us
comes only as we allow it by faith. God enables us
to pray as well as to have the faith to believe that
we have received that which we have asked of Him
according to His will.

God's Promises Are for Those
Who Fear God

It is an incredible thing to learn that God stands
behind His promises. His promises are exactly
like the laws of nature. When you throw a ball up
gravity pulls it down. It must happen and it
always will. God's promises are equally as
certain. When He makes a promise and we meet
the conditions of that promise, we can bank on the
fact the He will fulfill it. He has to. His Word
cannot fail to produce.

Paul wrote to Timothy, "If we believe not, yet he abideth faithful: he cannot deny himself" (II Timothy 2:13/KJ). Faith accepts God's promises and believes them. Paul said, "We know these things are true by believing, not by seeing" (II Corinthians 5:7).

Remember, "Jesus is the same yesterday, today and forever" (Hebrews 13:8). In Isaiah we read, "Surely he hath borne (removed at a distance) our grief (sickness) and carried our sorrows (diseases)" (Isaiah 53:4/KJ). God tells us in Proverbs, "For they (God's Words) are life to those that find them and health unto all their flesh" (Proverbs 4:22/KJ). The Hebrew word for health is "medicine." In the verse from Isaiah God has provided the abundant life for His children.

James wrote, "Is any sick among you? Let him call for the elders of the church and let them pray over him, anointing him with oil in the name of the Lord. And the prayer of faith shall save the sick and the Lord shall raise him up and if he has committed sins they shall be forgiven him" (James 5:14-15/KJ). God says, "They that seek the Lord shall not want any good thing" (Psalm 34:10). We are also assured, "The Lord is my shepherd, I shall not want" (Psalm 23:1/KJ).

The Bible says that the entrance of the Word gives light (Psalm 119:130). The devil will cause us to be blind to what God really says in order that he can keep us from walking in that light. Hosea wrote, "My people perish for lack of knowledge" (Hosea 4:6/KJ). We have not studied to fully understand and know what God has promised to us as believers and, therefore, we fail to receive the blessings God has for us. We must learn to

grab hold by faith and to receive the benefits of
God's Word. Abraham "staggered not at the
promise of God's word through unbelief; but was
strong in faith. . ." (Romans 4:20/KJ). We, too,
must have that kind of faith in God.

Reverence for God

It is needful for believers to understand something
of what it is to fear God. You will not walk in the
"rest" of God unless you walk in the "fear" of God.
This is not a frightful fear but a reverential awe
and respect for Him. The Bible says, "The fear of
God is to hate evil" (Proverbs 8:13). Many
Christians are lacking in this area. Solomon
wisely wrote, "In the fear of the Lord is strong
confidence: and his children shall have a place of
refuge. The fear of the Lord is a fountain of life, to
depart from the snares of death" (Proverbs 14:26-
27/KJ). He also wrote, "True humility and respect
for the Lord lead a man to riches, honor, and long
life" (Proverbs 22:4).

The Bible says, "As ye have therefore received
Christ Jesus the Lord, so walk ye in Him"
(Colossians 2:6/KJ). ". . .walk in the Spirit, and ye
shall not fulfill the lust of the flesh" (Galatians
5:16/KJ).

So many believers regard such a walk as
impossible that they do not feel it is a sin to walk
otherwise. They have become so accustomed to the
life of powerlessness that the life and walk in
God's strength has little attraction for them. It's
simply an unattainable ideal, but it is not! We dare
to enter into the very life of Jesus by the power of
His Spirit.

The Psalmist says, "Praise ye the Lord. Blessed is the man that feareth the Lord, that delighteth greatly in his commandments. His seed shall be mighty upon earth: the generation of the upright shall be blessed. Wealth and riches shall be in his house: and his righteousness endureth for ever" (Psalm 112:1-3/KJ).

What great promises to those who will fear the Lord. Our children and grandchildren who are taught to fear the Lord "shall be mighty upon the earth." All of our emotional, physical and material needs will be met in the promise, "wealth and riches shall be in his house." No need will lack His supply. Is it any wonder the Psalmist began this passage with, "Praise ye the Lord!" God keeps His Word.

All of the promises of God in Scripture, some 30,000 of them, are available to the child of God who will fear the Lord. In simplest terms, to "fear God" is to hate evil, refuse to have anything to do with it, turn from it and obey His Word. How much we miss because we do not apply this principle of walking in the fear of God.

Great power was released when Jesus came to His Father in prayer. When Jesus prayed, things happened. His disciples noticed this, and it changed their lives. When we go before God in prayer, we must believe Him for what He can do, and great things will happen in our lives too! Remember the instruction given in the book of Hebrews, "But without faith it is impossible to please him: for he that cometh to God must believe that he is, and that he is a rewarder of them that diligently seek him" (Hebrews 11:6/KJ).

Do not allow yourself to be discouraged in prayer. There is so much for us. All of the blessings promised to Abraham are ours for the claiming. However, only those who fear God, hate evil, and keep His commandments are those who can claim God's promises and who can expect to receive His blessings. Do we really fear God? If so, here are some of the blessings which are our rich inheritance:

In Proverbs we read, "Reverence for God gives a man deep strength; his children have a place of refuge and security. Reverence for the Lord is a fountain of life; its waters keep a man from death" (Proverbs 14:26-27).

The Psalmist wrote, "Praise the Lord! For all who fear God and trust in him are blessed beyond expression. Yes, happy is the man who delights in doing his commands.

"His children shall be honored everywhere, for good men's sons have a special heritage. He himself shall be wealthy, and his good deeds will never be forgotten. When darkness overtakes him, light will come bursting in. He is kind and merciful — and all goes well for the generous man who conducts his business fairly.

"Such a man will not be overthrown by evil circumstances. God's constant care of him will make a deep impression on all who see it. He does not fear bad news, nor live in dread of what may happen. For he is settled in his mind that Jehovah will take care of him. That is why he is not afraid, but can calmly face his foes. He gives generously to those in need. His deeds will never be forgotten. He shall have influence and honor" (Psalm 112:1-9).

In Deuteronomy we read, "The Lord will give you an abundance of good things in the land, just as he promised: many children, many cattle, and abundant crops. He will open to you his wonderful treasury of rain in the heavens, to give you fine crops every season. He will bless everything you do; and you shall lend to many nations, but shall not borrow from them. If you will only listen and obey the commandments of the Lord your God that I am giving to you today, he will make you the head and not the tail, and you shall always have the upper hand. But each of these blessings depends on your not turning aside in any way from the laws I have given you; and you must never worship other gods" (Deuteronomy 28:11-14). Solomon said, "If anyone respects and fears God, he will hate evil" (Proverbs 8:13). The righteousness of God is ours. Authority over the devil is ours. We truly have a very rich inheritance in Christ Jesus

> Every promise in the book is mine:
> Every chapter, every verse, every line;
> All the blessings of His love divine;
> Every promise in the book is mine.
> — Pearl Spencer Smith

It is often necessary for us to wait before the Lord. Sometimes there are long periods of time between our asking and our receiving the answer. Isaiah says, "But they that wait upon the Lord shall renew their strength; they shall mount up with wings as eagles; they shall run, and not be weary; and they shall walk, and not faint" (Isaiah 40:31/KJ).

Waiting in prayer for His leading is to be as the Psalmist wrote, "Be still, and know that I am God . . ." (Psalm 46:10a/KJ). We also must wait "expectantly" for God to answer. Again in Psalms we read, "My soul, wait thou only upon God; for my expectation is from him" (Psalm 62:5/KJ).

When our minds are settled upon God in prayer, we must not pray negatively. The right frame of mind is to have positive thoughts as we commune with Him in boldness and confidence. We are never to pray our problem. Always pray the answer. Pray in a positive frame of mind.

We must not allow ourselves to become discouraged when there is a delay in receiving answers to prayer or when we fail to find instant power. We sometimes must wait for answers so that our faith may be tested and strengthened and our power with God increased.

Pray for God to remove all obstacles and hindrances to faith. Discouragement comes when we look to our feelings rather than realizing we are dependent upon the deep working of the Holy Spirit within which is unseen and often unfelt.

If we do not yield to the control of the Spirit, He cannot work. We are not to be intimidated before our Lord. When asking has been done according to the will of God and His promises have been believed and accepted, know assuredly that God has answered. We must learn to live in the divine assurance and certainty of His answer based on His will and His Word. We determine to persevere — hold our confidence — until the answer comes, despite the difficulties and delays.

By faith claim the blessed assurance that God's abundant provision has been bestowed. By faith "see" the answer of God in your spirit as already having been received. By faith begin to act upon the answer. By faith accept His promises and stick with them until the answer becomes a reality. Exercise and strengthen faith through prayer at all times. By faith trust that God is working. By faith, know that the joy of the Lord is the source of strength.

Exercising Faith

What about faith? Everyone wants to know how to "get faith." Many talk about "getting more faith," or at least sufficient faith to make things happen. Faith is not something we find or muster up. Paul says, "Yet faith cometh by hearing and hearing by the Word of God" (Romans 10:17/KJV). Faith is not something we work for, it is a gift of God. This gift is given to every believer at salvation. It is already ours.

However, faith does have to be developed by exercising it. It is like learning to play the accordian. We learn to know where the notes are on the music and where they are on the keyboard. But then we actually begin to play the accordian as we exercise that which we know and put it into practice. So it is with faith. We increase our faith as we exercise it in our walk with God and in our obedience to Him.

We are often tested and tried in order that we might learn to pray and seek after God. Why do we stumble around in unbelief? We often cannot see any possible way for our needs to be met, yet God said He would provide. He has the answer to every problem we face already available for our taking.

Micah the prophet said, "As for me, I look to the Lord for His help; I wait for God to save me; He will hear me" (Micah 7:7).

God will provide for our needs. The faith for daily living is the same as for salvation. God was anxious to answer our prayer when as a sinner we called upon Him for salvation. How much more does He want to answer our prayers now that we are His children. We do not need to muster up faith or strive for great faith — we already have it. Just put it to the test. God will hear. He is waiting to grant our requests.

In Hebrews we read, "Now faith is being sure of what we hope for and certain of what we do not see. This is what the ancients were commended for" (Hebrews 11:1/NIV).

We exercise faith every day. I fly to many of my speaking engagements. When I board a plane, I do not question as to whether the mechanics serviced the plane properly or the ability of the pilots to navigate the plane. I just sit down in my seat, fasten my seat belt and wait for takeoff. It is the same with exercising faith. It is already there. I just use it!

We are to believe in our hearts and speak words of faith. Faith is power in our lives. The faith to remove mountains is the same as saving faith. By faith we come into the possession of things hoped for and prayed for. Faith is the link between God and man.

We need to develop a faith that's unmovable, steadfast and secure; a faith that will stand the test when mountains come into our lives. If we look to our own unworthiness and weakness, then we will be defeated and go down in despair. We must learn to conquer Satan. Paul wrote, "But despite all this, overwhelming victory is ours through Christ who loved us enough to die for us" (Romans 8:37). We need to use our God-given authority over fear and doubt. We must assume our rightful place and exercise our rights and authority which are ours because of our position in Christ. We read in II Corinthians, "For God took the sinless Christ and poured into Him our sins. Then, in exchange, He poured God's goodness into us" (II Corinthians 5:21).

Faith Is Proven By Works

James tells us, "So you see, it isn't enough just to have faith. You must also do good to prove that you have it. Faith that doesn't show itself by good works is no faith at all — it is dead and useless. But someone may well argue, 'You say the way to God is by faith alone, plus nothing; well, I say that good works are important too, for without good works you can't prove whether you have faith or not; but anyone can see that I have faith by the way I act.'

"Are there still some among you who hold that 'only believing' is enough? Believing in one God? Well, remember that the devils believe this too — so strongly that they tremble in terror! Dear foolish man! When will you ever learn that 'believing' is useless without doing what God wants you to? Faith that does not result in good deeds is not real faith" (James 2:17-20).

If we do not believe that we will receive what we asked for and act accordingly, then it will not come into reality. We must act upon our faith or our faith is dead. We are admonished in Hebrews, "Looking unto Jesus the author and finisher of our faith. . ." (Hebrews 12:2a/KJ). Applied to prayer, "author and finisher of our faith" simply means: God put the desire or need before us. He planted it in our spirit to begin working toward or praying for that desire or need. In that sense He is the "author" of it. He makes His desire, our desire, in order that we will pray and work toward the fulfillment of it. Then He also is the "finisher." He began the work in us. He put the desire there before us. Now, by faith, we are praying it through and working it out. He becomes the "finisher of our faith" as He makes that thing come to full reality.

We can be assured that God hears our prayers as we kneel before His throne asking for a definite request. From that moment on, we must believe that we have already received that which we and God have agreed upon in prayer. Our actions then must move toward the success of that for which we have prayed. The answer has already come, so we must move in that direction. We must lay the foundation, make preparation and do whatever is necessary to bring about the desired end.

Be A Non-Conformist

In Romans we read, "And be not conformed to this world: but be ye transformed by the renewing of your mind, that ye may prove what is that good, and acceptable, and perfect, will of God" (Romans 12:2/KJ). Our minds are renewed as they are fixed in the Word of God. We cannot live worldly lives and expect the blessings of God. In some ways this

verse has been misinterpreted. A quote taken from
Jerry Savells' book titled *Drawn By His Love* is as
follows: In the early days, the Church realized
that Christians shouldn't conform to the world, so
they tried their best not to look or talk or act like
the world. In their zeal not to conform, they
pushed non-conformity to the extreme. As a result
of their one-sided view, they did not make the
Gospel attractive. On the contrary, they gave the
world a very distorted picture of what a Christian
is supposed to look like and be. They presented an
image of poverty, ignorance and fanaticism which
was as unappealing as it was untrue.

"Such well-intentioned but sadly misinformed
Christians have tried so hard not to draw
attention to themselves that they stuck out like a
sore thumb. Such extremism does not adorn the
Gospel at all, it makes it look foolish and
repugnant.

"As a reaction against this kind of negative
presentation, many Christians have gone to the
opposite extreme. They have gone to great lengths
to adopt the world's ways, to imitate it, to cultivate
it. They are so afraid of appearing ignorant or
fanatical or out of step with the times, they have
adopted the world's values rather than remaining
true to God. They care more about appearance
than they do truth. In short, they are more
concerned with respectability than they are with
godliness.

"But just because people go from one extreme to
the other does not mean there is not a central
truth. And the truth is that although we
Christians are in the world, we are not of the

world. While we are to go into all the world and present to it a positive, attractive Gospel, we are not to be influenced by the world. We are not to be conformed to the world, we are to conform it to the image of Jesus Christ.

"As Christians we ought to always be 'on our best behavior' so to speak. We ought always to strive to present to people, whatever their station in life, a pleasant and attractive image. As Christ's ambassadors, we represent the King of Kings. We ought to make certain we do a good job of representing Christ so that others will be attracted to come to know Him too."

We are in the world but we are not of the world. We must appropriate the power of the Holy Spirit within us to overcome the world and all its appeal. As we have intimate fellowship with God, He will reveal His power in and through us.

James tells us, "And when you draw close to God, God will draw close to you" (James 4:8a). In other words, greater strength will be available to overcome the world, the lust of the flesh and the Devil. Inwardly, as we focus on Jesus, the words of the chorus of *Turn Your Eyes Upon Jesus* will be true:

> Turn your eyes upon Jesus,
> Look full in His wonderful face,
> And the things of earth will grow strangely dim
> In the light of His glory and grace.

The more we struggle against a particular sin in our lives, the more we will be drawn to it. Our concentration must not be on the sin but rather on Jesus. We cannot think about sin and Jesus at the same time. The Psalmist wrote, "I am always thinking of the Lord; and because he is so near, I never need to stumble or to fall. My heart, body and soul are filled with joy" (Psalm 16:8-9). John declares, "But if we are living in the light of God's presence, just as Christ does, then we have wonderful fellowship and joy with each other, and the blood of Jesus His Son cleanses us from every sin" (I John 1:7). In Proverbs we read, ". . . blessings chase the righteous" (Proverbs 13:21b).

Be Skilled In The Word

Our skills in the use of the Word of God must be sharpened in order to deal with the devil. He cannot stand up against the Bible. Each of the three times Satan tempted Jesus in the wilderness, Jesus responded, "It is written." Jesus used the Scriptures to defeat Satan. When Satan tempts us, we must immediately utilize the "Word" of God, the "sword" of the Spirit, and he will flee from us. Satan will flee when resisted with the Word of God. What incredible power is available to those who will believe.

The "gifts of the Spirit" which God gave to the church are not optional. We are not given a choice to accept or reject them. We are told to use them. Paul said, ". . .Stir up the gift that is in you. . ." (II Timothy 1:6). How often have we missed God's mighty power working in our midst because we have quenched the Spirit by not doing all God commands us to do? The gifts are our weapons in spiritual battle.

Remember the words of Paul, "Last of all I want to remind you that your strength must come from the Lord's mighty power within you. Put on all of God's armor so that you will be able to stand safe against all strategies and tricks of Satan. For we are not fighting against people made of flesh and blood, but against persons without bodies — the evil rulers of the unseen world, those mighty satanic beings and great evil princes of darkness who rule this world; and against huge numbers of wicked spirits in the spirit world. So use every piece of God's armor to resist the enemy whenever he attacks, and when it is all over, you will still be standing up.

"But to do this, you will need the strong belt of truth and the breastplate of God's approval. Wear shoes that are able to speed you on as you preach the Good News of peace with God. In every battle you will need faith as your shield to stop the fiery arrows aimed at you by Satan. And you will need the helmet of salvation and the sword of the Spirit — which is the Word of God. Pray all the time. Ask God for anything in line with the Holy Spirit's wishes. Plead with Him, reminding Him of your needs, and keep praying earnestly for all Christians everywhere" (Ephesians 6:10-18).

Forgiveness and cleansing are available to us in the blood of Christ. The words of the hymn *Power in the Blood* by Lewis E. Jones say:

Would you be free from the burden of sin?
There's pow'r in the blood, pow'r in the blood;
Would you o'er evil a victory win?
There's wonderful pow'r in the blood.

The words of the fourth verse of the hymn *O for a Thousand Tongues* by Charles Wesley are:

He breaks the pow'r of canceled sin,
He sets the pris'ner free;
His blood can make the foulest clean —
His blood availed for me.

It is only the blood of Jesus Christ that can break
the power of sin. Sin holds us captive but the blood
of Christ sets us free. Praise God!

Intimacy with God Insures Growth

The secret to spiritual progress is to have a desire
to know God's wisdom in directing our growth.
The Psalmist wrote, "As the deer pants for water,
so I long for you, O God. I thirst for God, the living
God. Where can I find him to come and stand
before him?" (Psalm 42:1-2). We need to have a
strong yearning in our soul that pants after
righteousness. In her beautiful hymn *Satisfied*
Clare Williams wrote:

All my life long I had panted
For a drink from some cool spring
That I hoped would quench the burning
Of the thirst I felt within.

Chorus
Hallelujah! I have found Him
Whom my soul so long has craved!
Jesus satisfies my longings;
Through His blood I now am saved.

Calvary Dealt with the Sins of All Time

If God had taken care of only our past through the
death of His Son on Calvary, we would have no

forgiveness or cleansing for daily living which would leave us with nothing but defeat and despair. But when Christ was crucified, we were crucified with Him. God laid on Jesus every sin that every person in the world would ever commit— past sins, present sins and future sins. All believers, those who have trusted Christ as personal Savior, were crucified with Christ nearly 2,000 years ago.

The crucifixion of Christ provided payment for the penalty of all sins for all time. Now Christians can live a life "dead unto sin." Paul says, "Your old evil desires were nailed to the cross with Him; that part of you that loves to sin was crushed and fatally wounded, so that your sin-loving body is no longer under sin's control, no longer needs to be a slave to sin;

"For when you are deadened to sin you are freed from all its allure and its power over you. And since your old sin-loving nature 'died' with Christ, we know that you will share His new life" (Romans 6:6-8). What a promise! We may not always feel like that really happened to us, but feelings do not change the fact.

We accept the things God wants to give to us by faith. Jesus said, "Listen to Me! You can pray for anything, and if you believe, you have it; it's yours" (Mark 11:24). "Believing that you have received" is essential in gaining answers to our prayers. First we seek the mind of God regarding our desires, making sure our desires are in accordance with His will; then by faith through the Holy Spirit within us, knowing that God is faithful to keep His promises, our answer is forthcoming.

We must not allow fear and doubt to keep us from receiving all that is our inheritance in Christ — the eternal riches of His glory and the abundance of things hoped for. Paul wrote, "Don't worry about anything; instead, pray about everything; tell God your needs and don't forget to thank Him for His answers. If you do this you will experience God's peace, which is far more wonderful than the human mind can understand, His peace will keep your thoughts and your hearts quiet and at rest as you trust in Christ Jesus" (Philippians 4:6-7). When we are at peace that God has answered our prayers, we need to stay with it.

Our confidence must be in Him. John wrote, "And we are sure of this, that He will listen to us whenever we ask Him for anything in line with His will. And if we really know He is listening when we talk to Him and make our requests, then we can be sure that He will answer us" (I John 5:14-15).

In Hebrews we read, "You can never please God without faith, without depending on Him. Anyone who wants to come to God must believe that there is a God and that He rewards those who sincerely look for Him" (Hebrews 11:6). Our requests will not be answered if we do not confidently depend upon Him. There is great recompense of reward for holding our confidence — faith — a belief that God is going to fulfill His promises to us. We know, we are assured in our spirit, that God has heard our prayer. Faith is simple. Just dare to believe God. He knows when the righteous cry. James wrote, "If you don't ask with faith, don't expect the Lord to give you any solid answer" (James 1:6-8).

Chapter Nine
Hindrances to Faith

Negative Input

A REAL HINDRANCE to our faith and prayer life is that of possessing a judgmental, critical spirit. God says, "Judge not that ye be not judged" (Matthew 7:1/KJ).

"A worthless man devises and digs up mischief and in his lips there is a scorching fire" (Proverbs 16:7). "Devises" means to assassinate another person's character, motives or lifestyle. Again in Proverbs we read, "A worthless person, a wicked man walks with a perverse mouth. Perversity is in his heart. He deviseth evil continuously. He sows discord. He speaks critical things, deviseth trouble, vexation and evil" (Proverbs 6:12, 14/KJ).

Satan causes one to always look for flaws and weaknesses in others and then give negative input. When we speak negative talk here and there, others pick it up and pass it on. Sowing discord among the brethren is a trap of Satan. After awhile it explodes and is blown all out of proportion. The end result is disastrous and causes divisions. God says this person is

worthless and his feet are swift to run to evil. This
one has a spirit that is completely against God. He
is unspiritual at that moment because he is not
acting according to the Spirit. His heart is open to
Satanic intervention. God's judgment will fall
upon those who are guilty of doing this and that
person can look forward to problems and conflicts
in his own life. Why? Because he has given in to
the devil's snare. In verse 15 we read, "Therefore
his calamity shall come suddenly, suddenly he
shall be broken without remedy."

We must confess this great sin and turn from it.
Take authority over the devil and defeat him in the
Name of Jesus. God calls those who do these
things "evil doers." In Proverbs we read, "A
gentle tongue (with it's healing power) is a tree of
life, but willful contrariness in it breaks down the
spirit" (Proverbs 15:4). Peter wrote, ". . .your
adversary the devil, as a roaring lion, walketh
about, seeking whom he may devour" (I Peter
5:8/KJ).

When we have perceived in our heart the wrong
someone is up to, we must not speak of it openly,
but rather go to God in prayer over it. The one who
through the Spirit and power of God is able to
control his tongue is highly matured in
possessing the nature of Christ. He has learned to
bridle his tongue and the life of Jesus can flow
through his life. My husband has learned to bridle
his tongue. He has the nature of Christ flowing
through him and God uses him greatly.

In Proverbs we are told, "A happy heart is a good
medicine and a cheerful mind works healing, but
a broken spirit dries the bones" (Proverbs 17:22).

This verse implies that a judgmental spirit dries out the bones. Could this be a cause of arthritis?

Generally when one is always looking for the bad in others, it's because he is feeling insecure in his own abilities. Thus it shows one's weakness. "Sweet water will not flow from a bitter well."

Negative Words

God says, "We are snared by the words of our mouth" (Proverbs 6:2). The more we are controlled by the inner Spirit of God, the less we will make a negative confession. We also read in Proverbs, "Death and life are in the power of the tongue" (Proverbs 18:4), and "A man shall eat the fruit of his mouth" (Proverbs 13:2).

When we criticize ourselves, we open the door for Satan to do that very thing we have spoken. We may say many things we should not speak, such as: "we're getting that age, you know, when we have to be concerned about high blood pressure and heart problems," or "I'm afraid my little Susie is not going to like school this year," or "My arthritis is just moving everywhere, all over my body." It will. You just gave power to it. We say things we don't desire, yet we speak things into motion.

We do the same thing in prayer. We pray the problem rather than the answer and therefore, the situation can only get worse. Mark wrote, "Whosoever shall say to this mountain, be thou removed and be thou cast into the sea, and shall not doubt in his heart, but shall believe that those things which he saith shall come to pass, he shall have whatever he saith" (Mark 11:23/KJ). God's Word holds true. We will have what we say.

It can be noticed in the atmosphere of a church. If people are happy and talking about the great things God is doing among them—how God is blessing in the attendance and finances of the church—that church shall be continually blessed. However, in a church where there is a defeatist attitude and people are being critical of this and that, talking about how the church is not growing and of the money problems that exist, and how it is just not going to make it, that church will not know the blessing of God. The Spirit is quenched. Satan has an open door to come in and cause things to happen just as people said it would.

Rise up. Break the cords that bind. Take back those negative words and take authority over Satan. Defeat him by the power of God and in the name of Jesus. We can do great and mighty things for God!

Learn to speak words that edify and build up. Speak to bring down God's blessings, and not the curse. Build yourself up in the most holy faith. Speak positively about your family, the church, friends, your place of work, your health and finances. God wants to bless you, but Satan has you in bondage by the words of your own mouth.

Indecent Language

Another hindrance to our faith is that of indecent language. Slang expressions bring us into the realm of Satan. One cannot walk in the Spirit while speaking blessing and cursing out of the same mouth.

Proverbs says, "Willful contrariness breaks down the spirit" (Proverbs 15:26). The mouth of the wicked pours out evil things. Indecent language destroys the inner working of the Spirit, your personality, and soul. It brings oppression. Your words bring death or life to the spirit within you.

In Ephesians we read, "Strip yourselves of your former nature. Put off or discard your old unrenewed self which characterized your previous manner of life" (Ephesians 4:22). Verse 29 continues, "Let no foul or polluted language, nor evil word, unwholesome worthless talk ever come out of your mouth but such (speech) as is fitting to the need and the occasion, that it may be a blessing and give grace (God's favor) to those who hear it."

Unforgiveness

We exercise faith simply by daring to believe God. We must dare to believe that He will hear us and that He will answer. However, often our prayers are hindered because of our "lack of forgiveness" toward another person, or our need to ask their forgiveness for something we said or did to them. D. L. Moody once said, "Those who say they will forgive but can't forget, simply bury the hatchet, but leave the handle out for immediate use."

Many Christians are guilty of incomplete forgiveness. We say that we have forgiven someone, but inside we really didn't want to and in essence have not. Forgiveness does not take place unless the offense doesn't bother us anymore. Jesus taught us that if we do not forgive others, neither will God forgive us. In His Sermon

on the Mount Jesus said, "Your heavenly Father
will forgive you if you forgive those who sin
against you; but if you refuse to forgive them, He
will not forgive you" (Matthew 6:14-15).

Forgiving others is very important. The most
effective way to be able to forgive someone is to
pray for them daily, asking God to bless them in
specific ways. Even though you don't want to do
this, do it. It's hard, but bless them until you gain
the victory. It will work, and you also will be
blessed.

Anger

The sin of anger stored up and held in the heart
can hinder prayer. Paul wrote: "If you are angry,
don't sin by nursing your grudge. Don't let the
sun go down with you still angry — get over it
quickly; For when you are angry you give a mighty
foothold to the devil" (Ephesians 4:26-27). When
you express your anger through violent language,
you are not presenting yourself as a living
sacrifice to God. Satan has a hold on you and has
caused you to lose your oneness in the Spirit. In
Proverbs we read, "The uncompromising
righteous study how to answer" (Proverbs 28:28).
As Christians we can be calm in our spirit,
having our personality consumed by the flow of
Christ's nature through us.

Sometimes anger is necessary and the right way
to react. It is possible for us to be angry and not to
sin. Jesus was angry when He threw the money
changers out of the temple. He expressed
righteous, controlled anger. It was directed

toward sin and He had a definite plan of action through which to channel it.

Jealousy

Another hindrance to prayer is the sin of "jealousy." Solomon said, "Jealousy is as cruel as Sheol. It flashes fire, the very flame of Jehovah" (Song of Solomon 8:6b). These are strong words. Jealousy occurs when one feels weak and insecure—usually in areas where one does not accept himself. It is a trap from Satan. It must be confessed and forsaken. Jealousy consumes us and hinders our prayers.

Intimidation

The sin of intimidation is often overlooked. It is wrong both to be intimidated and to intimidate. The Psalmist David said, "The Lord is my light and my salvation; he protects me from danger — whom shall I fear?" (Psalm 27:1). To be intimidated is to be afraid. Fear is not of God. The Christian need not live under the dark cloud of intimidation for "the Lord is his light." The Christian is a child of the King and rightfully can take his place as such.

Likewise, Christians are not to intimidate others, striking fear into them. Paul says, "Don't be selfish; don't live to make a good impression on others. Be humble, thinking of others as better than yourself" (Philippians 2:3). Intimidation of either kind can hinder our prayers.

Worldly Desires

We read in I John, "Stop loving this evil world and
all that it offers you, for when you love these
things you show that you do not really love God;
For all these worldly things, these evil desires —
the craze for sex, the ambition to buy everything
that appeals to you, and the pride that comes from
wealth and importance — these are not from God.
They are from this evil world itself. And this
world is fading away, and these evil, forbidden
things will go with it, but whoever keeps doing the
will of God will live forever" (I John 2:15-17).

In Proverbs it says, "Everyone who is proud in
heart is an abomination to the Lord" (Proverbs
16:5). The Spirit of God can not flow through a
personality that's proud, sophisticated and stiff.
We must deal with our sin before we can expect
God to hear and answer our prayers.

Dare to Believe God

If God tells us to do something, we should just do
it. Godliness is within our reach because we
possess the life of Christ. If we are always
wrapped up in thinking about our old nature and
paying attention to it, it becomes more and more
active. Self-discipline and self-denial are
necessary to decrease our desires for sin and
wrong. We must take our minds off our sins and
turn them inward to focus on God's deliverance.
As we turn our thoughts to the new man within
in Christ, then the old man will become weaker
and weaker. Fires which are not kindled will die.

Abandon ourselves to the Lord and He will make us strong.

Begin each new day by saying, "Oh Jesus, I love You, I love You, I love You." Rejoice in the God of your salvation. Allow His warm, tender presence to flood your soul. Pray with the Psalmist, "How I love your laws! How I enjoy your commands! 'Come, come to me.' I call to them, for I love them and will let them fill my life. Never forget your promises to me your servant, for they are my only hope. They give me strength in all my troubles; how they refresh and revive me" (Psalm 119:47-50). "Stand ready to help me because I have chosen to follow your will" (Psalm 119:173). Quote Scripture to God and He will honor His Word.

Many Christians cover their sins by saying, "I have no convictions against this. Just because you think it is sin doesn't make it sin for me." The Holy Spirit does not have two sets of standards. He will not tell one Christian that what he is doing is right and tell another the same practice is wrong. Sin is sin, right is right, wrong is wrong for every believer. There is no double standard with God. However, we believers are not to judge one another regarding these matters, because each of us knows that that which we will regard to be sin in our individual lives will vary according to the knowledge we have of God's Word. We are only accountable to God for that which we know and understand to be good or evil.

Realize that God never takes away our free will. We have many choices to make and He will not make us do anything against our will. When our spirit loses contact with God, we are as dead. It is up to us to pursue God personally and individually.

We must ask the question, "Do I desire to know the Lord and to have a deep, close fellowship with Him?" This is possible for us as we are sensitive to the presence of the Holy Spirit within us. We must be cautious not to grieve Him. We can do this by failing to be sensitive to the prompting of His voice to our spirit. We need to recognize His promptings and conviction as the very power of God working within us. The Holy Spirit will reveal Himself to us daily in many ways. We must accept Him and His presence as He communicates within us. We must accept His leading and wooing, respond to Him in love and unquenchable faith and trust Him to do all that He says He will do for He cannot lie. Talk to the Holy Spirit when you are alone. Don't just ignore Him. Learn to know what grieves Him, what makes Him angry. He is a person who hurts, responds, perceives, speaks, comforts, and loves. He wants to be loved. He desires our fellowship but He will not force Himself upon us unless we invite Him to do so. He desires to do so much for us. He is the power of the Godhead.

Jeremiah wrote, "Call to Me, and I will answer you, and I will tell you great and mighty things, which you do not know" (Jeremiah 33:3/NAS). In Ephesians we read, "Now glory be to God who by His mighty power at work within us is able to do far more than we would ever dare to ask or even dream of — infinitely beyond our highest prayers, desires, thoughts, or hopes" (Ephesians 3:20). When we doubt Him and do not trust Him, the problem is with us, not with Him. May we learn to reverence God and to trust Him completely.

It can all be summed up in this: stay away from anything that breaks the line of communication and fellowship with our Lord. Sin not only breaks the line of communication and fellowship with the Lord, but it also can bring His judgment. Solomon says, "How does a man become wise? The first step is to trust and reverence the Lord! Only fools refuse to be taught" (Proverbs 1:7). It is vital for us to develop a healthy respect of God for Who He is and be aware that His blessings and the answers to our prayers will be withheld when sin is present in our lives.

As Christians we need to know how God views sin in our lives and how He will deal with it. The writer to the Hebrews says, "And have you quite forgotten the encouraging words God spoke to you, His child? He said, 'My son, don't be angry when the Lord punishes you. Don't be discouraged when He has to show you where you are wrong. For when He punishes you, it proves He loves you. When He whips you it proves you are really His child.' Let God train you, for He is doing what any loving father does for his children.

"Whoever heard of a son who was never corrected? If God doesn't punish you when you need it, as other fathers punish their sons, then it means that you aren't really God's son at all — that you don't really belong in His family. . . .Being punished isn't enjoyable while it is happening — it hurts! But afterwards we can see the result, a quiet growth in grace in character" (Hebrews 12:5-8, 11).

God's Blessings Bestowed

God's blessings are promised to those who fear Him, obey Him and keep His commandments. In Proverbs we read, "He who fears the Lord has a secure fortress, and for his children it will be a refuge. The fear of the Lord is a fountain of life, turning a man from the snares of death (Proverbs 14:26-27/NIV). Psalm 112 assures the person who fears God that he will have a strong family; his descendants will be mighty upon the earth; he will know no want; no good thing will be withheld from him; he can be generous in his giving for wealth and riches will be his; he will be gracious, compassionate and righteous in character; he will not fear evil news; his heart will be steadfast and he will be contented in life.

Moses said, "If you fully obey the Lord your God and carefully follow all his commands I give you today, the Lord will set you high above all the nations on earth. All these blessings will come upon you and accompany you if you obey the Lord your God: You will be blessed in the city and blessed in the country. The fruit of your womb will be blessed, the crops of your land and the young of your livestock — the calves of your herds and the lambs of your flocks. Your basket and your kneading trough will be blessed. You will be blessed when you come in and when you go out" (Deuteronomy 28:1-6/NIV).

Bill Gothard has said, "The fear of God is the continued awareness that I am in the presence of a holy, just and almighty God. Every thought, word, action and deed is open before Him and is being judged by Him." It is necessary for us to get back to basics. Peter said, "Therefore, rid yourselves of all malice and all deceit, hypocrisy, envy, and slander of every kind. Like newborn babies, crave pure spiritual milk, so that by it you may grow up in your salvation, now that you have tasted that the Lord is good" (I Peter 2:1-2/NIV). Every minute detail of our lives must be examined in the light of the Word of God.

The words of the hymn *Rock of Ages* really speak to me. I trust that they will speak to you also.

Rock of Ages, cleft for me,
Let me hide myself in Thee;
Let the water and the blood,
From Thy wounded side which flowed,
Be of sin the double cure:
Save from wrath and make me pure.

Could my tears forever flow,
Could my zeal no respite know,
This for sin could not atone —
Thou must save, and Thou alone:
In my hand no price I bring,
Simply to Thy cross I cling.
When I draw my final breath,
When my eyes shall close in death,
When I rise to worlds unknown
And behold Thee on Thy throne,
Rock of Ages, cleft for me,
Let me hide myself in Thee.
— A. M. Toplady

We need to learn what it is to hide ourselves in Jesus Christ and rest in Him as the firm

foundation of our faith. The grand hymn from the
1700s, *How Firm a Foundation,* whose author is
unknown, is one of my favorites. Read it carefully.
Meditate upon its words.

How firm a foundation, ye saints of the Lord,
Is laid for your faith in His excellent Word!
What more can He say than to you He hath said —
To you, who for refuge to Jesus have fled?

Fear not, I am with thee — O be not dismayed,
For I am thy God, I will still give thee aid;
I'll strengthen thee, help thee,
and cause thee to stand,
Upheld by my gracious, omnipotent hand.

When thru the deep waters I call thee to go,
The rivers of woe shall not thee overflow;
For I will be with thee thy troubles to bless,
And sanctify to thee thy deepest distress.

When thru fiery trials thy pathway shall lie,
My grace, all sufficient, shall be thy supply;
The flame shall not hurt thee — I only design
Thy dross to consume and thy gold to refine.

The soul that on Jesus hath leaned for repose,
I will not, I will not desert to his foes;
That soul, tho all hell should endeavor to shake,
I'll never — no never — no never forsake!

These words really say it all. Our God is with us
and will never forsake us. Praise the Lord! May
we never allow sin to hinder our prayers to God. A

saying quoted earlier needs to be kept in mind when we submit to self-examination: "If you feel far from God, guess who moved." We must go to our knees in prayer, confess our sins, draw near to God and feel His loving arms embrace us as we draws near to Him.

Chapter Ten
A Hunger for God

ALL CHRISTIANS have a built-in hunger system to know intimate fellowship with God and to know more about Him through His Word. Spiritual hunger pangs for God are the same as those for physical food. Jesus said, "Blessed (*spiritually prosperous*) are they which do hunger and thirst after righteousness: for they shall be filled" (Matthew 5:6/KJ - italics mine).

When we come to the knowledge of how to lay hold of God in prayer, we become so overjoyed with this new enlightenment of the Holy Spirit as He reveals Himself to us that we do not have any more trouble desiring to pray. As with the force of a magnet, the Holy Spirit draws us to Himself. His love is so compelling that we cannot wait to spend precious time alone with God. Our very souls are turned inward toward Him enabling us to enjoy Christ's presence throughout the day. And as we learn more and more to wait before Him, there is nothing like it, for we are drawn deeper and deeper into the love of Jesus. We desire to engage in persevering prayer just to see His power brought down to us. We lay everything else aside to make time to spend with Him.

We begin to understand the meaning of the fact
that Christ is truly our life. We also begin to
comprehend the grief He feels when we do not
trust Him completely. We are to be so steadfast in
His love that nothing can move us as we say, "I
just can't get enough of Jesus."

Outward distractions can cause us to stray away
from this oneness in Christ but He will give us the
ability in our spirit to seek His presence. This is
accomplished through the use of Scripture as we
look to Him. Our hearts will know the love that
flows from Him to us. Then, as we are drawn by
His Spirit to live in His presence, we'll not want to
drift away from Him. This new desire within us is
of Him. We are now under the control of His
power and our souls are following His Spirit. It is
vital that we yield ourselves completely to Him as
He works in our hearts.

There are some days when I must get up at 5:00
in the morning to catch a flight to a speaking
engagement. When I have to leave for the airport
that early in the morning, I am in such a big
hurry that I put off having my quiet time with the
Lord. I do pray as I drive to the airport and while
on the plane, but during such a day my heart
aches and longs for the hour when I can be alone
with God in my motel room and earnestly seek His
fellowship through Bible study and prayer.

Reverence God

We need to become as conscious of the reality of
God's presence in our lives as is the presence of a
friend. We need to sense His presence with us at
all times. We can sense when someone enters a

room, even though we may not have seen them. So it is with God. We must learn to sense His presence as we are in church, at school, at work, at home, or wherever we may be. As we learn to joy in His fellowship, His presence will strengthen us. Of the many experiences we may have with our Lord, this one is the most important and ought never to cease. As we are in His presence, His love will flow through us to others like rivers of water.

When we are new babes in Christ, we sense His presence in prayer and in worship services. As we mature, we know Jesus Himself is praying in and through us continually. This blessed discovery keeps us aware of Him at all times. As we allow the Lord to control our lives totally, sensing His presence within becomes very natural. When we abandon everything, our entire existence to God, we recognize that everything that happens in our lives is in His control. His Spirit completely encompasses our souls (mind, will and emotions). We learn that we remain in His presence no matter where we go or what we do. Our sweet fellowship with Him then remains unbroken. We cannot arrive at this through self-effort, but only through total surrender to Him. As we pray for His enlightenment, He will reveal many deep things to us.

The Scripture asks the question, "Where is the man who fears the Lord? God will teach him how to choose the best" (Psalm 25:12). Those who have a reverential respect for God are those whom He will teach in His ways. These are the men who will live within the circle of God's blessings. David instructs us, "Mark this well: The Lord has set

apart the redeemed for himself. Therefore he will
listen to me and answer when I call to him. Stand
before the Lord in awe, and do not sin against
him . . ." (Psalm 4:3-4a).

Worship God

Worship is essential to real prayer. The Psalmist
says, "O magnify the Lord with me, and let us
exalt his name together" (Psalm 34:3/KJV).
Intimate fellowship with God comes to us when
we magnify Him for Who He is, as well as for all
He has done, is doing and will do for us. The
Christian is richly blessed who meditates on the
wonder of it all that "Jesus loves me!"

David also said, "For the Angel of the Lord
guards and rescues all who reverence him. . . . If
you belong to the Lord, reverence him; for
everyone who does this has everything he needs. .
. . The good man does not escape all troubles — he
has them too. But the Lord helps him in each and
every one" (Psalm 34:7, 9, 19). It is not that we will
never be sick or have difficulties, but when we do,
God is there to deliver us.

David declared, "But give great joy to all who
wish me well. Let them shout with delight, 'Great
is the Lord who enjoys helping his child!' And I
will tell everyone how great and good you are; I
will praise you all day long" (Psalm 35:27-28).

As everything we do is entrusted to the Lord, He
has promised His provision for our needs. What
does it mean to be delighted with the Lord? It
simply means that we find our pleasure in
obeying Him.

Praise God

I believe that the ultimate praise to God is to be found in the clapping and lifting up of holy hands. In Psalms we read, "O clap your hands, all ye people; shout unto God with the voice of triumph" (Psalm 47:1/KJ). Isaiah tells us, "For ye shall go out with joy, and be led forth with peace: the mountains and the hills shall break forth before you into singing, and all the trees of the field shall clap their hands" (Isaiah 55:12/KJ). Certainly if the trees of the fields are pictured as applauding God with their leaves and branches, should we do less? "Lift up your hands in the sanctuary and bless the Lord" (Psalm 134:2/KJ). I sincerely believe that these words should be taken literally.

The Psalmist also says, "Let the sea in all its vastness roar with praise! Let the earth and all those living on it shout, 'Glory to the Lord'" (Psalm 98:7-8). David also wrote, "Praise him for the growing fields, for they display his greatness. Let the trees of the forest rustle with praise" (Psalm 96:12). Since God deserves our highest praise, the clapping of our hands is right to do, whether in a church service or somewhere alone. Paul said: "I will therefore that men pray every where, lifting up holy hands, without wrath and doubting" (I Timothy 2:8/KJ). Believers ought to be the happiest people on planet earth and should express that happiness in exuberant praise to the Lord. So clap your hands!

God desires that we live our lives in constant glory, praise and honor, both to Him and for Him. In Psalms we find, "What I want from you is your true thanks; I want your promises fulfilled. I want you to trust me in your times of trouble, so I

can rescue you, and you can give me glory"
(Psalm 50:14-15).

Psalm 96 says, "Sing a new song to the Lord!
Sing it everywhere around the world! Sing out his
praises! Bless his name! Each day tell someone
that he saves" (Psalm 96:1-2). If we enjoy lifting
our voices in praise to the Lord now, what will it
be like when we're at home in heaven with Him?
It is beyond our comprehension.

It is important for us to learn how to bless
(praise) the Lord by bringing into remembrance
the glorious things He has done for us. Many
Psalms contain lists of praise items. Look at some
of the things David listed in Psalm 103: "I bless the
holy name of God with all my heart. Yes, I will
bless the Lord and not forget the glorious things
he does for me.

"He forgives all my sins. He heals me. He
ransoms me from hell. He surrounds me with
lovingkindness and tender mercies! He fills my
life with good things! My youth is renewed like the
eagle's! He gives justice to all who are treated
unfairly. He revealed his will and nature to Moses
and the people of Israel.

"He is merciful and tender toward those who
don't deserve it; he is slow to get angry and full of
kindness and love. He never bears a grudge, nor
remains angry forever. He has not punished us as
we deserve for all our sins, for his mercy toward
those who fear and honor him is as great as the
height of the heavens above the earth. He has
removed our sins as far away from us as the east
is from the west. He is like a father to us, tender
and sympathetic to those who reverence him"
(Psalm 103:1-13). This Psalm of David provides a

pattern for us to use when we express our praise to the Lord for all He has done for us.

An anonymous writer has expressed it like this:

> O God, how great You are.
> How You are robed with honor
> and majesty and light
> You stretch forth Your starry curtains
> through the heavens
> and the clouds are your chariots.
> You ride upon the wings of the wind
> and the angels are your messengers.
> The vast oceans are Your bed
> as well as the mountains
> that rise up from the valleys that sink.

Persevere with God

In our spiritual walk with the Lord, we must develop perseverance. Perseverance does not come to us by asking and receiving. Through the Word, God chisels and chips away those things in our lives which hinder our spiritual development. James says, "Consider it pure joy, my brothers, whenever you face trials of many kinds, because you know that the testing of your faith develops perseverance. Perseverance must finish its work so that you may be mature and complete, not lacking anything" (James 1:2-4/NIV).

Jesus prayed three times in the Garden of Gethsemane that if there were any other way to bring salvation to mankind other than the cross, that the Father would release Him from its suffering. He prayed, ". . . My Father! If it is possible, let this cup be taken away from Me. But I want Your will, not Mine" (Matthew 26:39b).

Jesus suffered and was tempted as we are, but He overcame these temptations by the Word. So we are to speak the Word when we go through suffering and temptation. We claim the victory through the use of God's Word. There's power in the Word. Learn to use it boldly.

Someone has said, "There's nothing God and I can't handle together." Paul assures us, "No temptation has seized you except what is common to man. And God is faithful; he will not let you be tempted beyond what you can bear. But when you are tempted, he will also provide a way out so that you can stand up under it" (I Corinthians 10:13/NIV). "Put on the whole armor of God that ye may be able to stand against the wiles of the devil. . . . Put on the breastplate of righteousness. . . . Use the sword of the Spirit, which is the Word of God, and defeat Satan." (Ephesians 6:11, 14b, 17b/KJ).

Flesh Control or God Control?

Paul tells us, "For they that are after the flesh do mind the things of the flesh; but they that are after the Spirit the things of the Spirit . . . . So then they that are in the flesh cannot please God" (Romans 8:5, 8/KJ).

Watchman Nee explains that, "The flesh can not only produce sin, it can also produce good by doing righteous deeds. If the flesh is what's doing the good that we do, then the flesh is yet alive. The good of the flesh is not one bit more presentable than the evil side, for both pertain to the flesh. So by letting the flesh do good — it is doing evil."

The Church at Corinth was made up of a group of people who were rich in knowledge, who knew their doctrine and who were learned in prophecy. However, their understanding was only in their minds. They had learned well all that they were taught. Yet they taught and preached to others while they themselves were unspiritual. Paul said, "Dear brothers, I have been talking to you as though you were still just babies in the Christian life, who are not following the Lord, but your own desires; I cannot talk to you as I would to healthy Christians, who are filled with the Spirit. I have had to feed you with milk and not with solid food, because you couldn't digest anything stronger. And even now you still have to be fed on milk" (I Corinthians 3:1-2).

Many times that which we begin in the Spirit, we terminate unfortunately in the flesh. In Galatians we read, "Are ye so foolish? having begun in the Spirit, are ye now made perfect by the flesh?" (Galatians 3:3/KJ). In other words, our righteous acts can actually be unrighteous deeds. Good works that are performed in the power of the flesh are an abomination to God. Paul says, ". . . we who worship by the Spirit of God, who glory in Christ Jesus, are to put no confidence in the flesh. . . (Philippians 3b/NIV). Some people have charisma and much self-confidence today, but God says, "Put no confidence in the flesh." Our sufficiency must be in Christ and His wonder-working power.

Christ Our Confidence

Our confidence must be in our relationship with Jesus Christ our Lord. We read in Jeremiah, "But blessed is the man who trusts in the Lord and has made the Lord his hope and confidence" (Jeremiah 17:7).

Paul prayed for the Ephesians, "That He would grant you, according to the riches of His glory, to be strengthened with power through His Spirit in the inner man: so that Christ may dwell in your hearts through faith: and that you, being rooted and grounded in love, may be able to comprehend with all the saints what is the breadth and length and height and depth, and to know the love of Christ which surpasses knowledge, that you may be filled up to all the fulness of God" (Ephesians 3:16-19/NAS).

Our hunger for God is satisfied as we fellowship with Him in prayer and in the study of His Word. Our spirits will be strengthened as we grow to maturity in Christ. Victory over the sins of the flesh will be ours as we confidently put our complete trust in Him.

If somehow I could only have the ability to convince my fellow believers to seek the power of God in their lives and to realize that God does desire to reveal the hidden treasures of His Word to them, together we'd be able to turn the world upside down. Then the words of the model prayer given to us by Jesus would become real in our lives: ". . . Thy will be done in earth, as it is in heaven" (Matthew 6:10b/KJ). We need to lay hold of and claim the unction of the Holy Spirit in our lives.

Jesus said, "Blessed are they which do hunger and thirst after righteousness: for they shall be filled" (Matthew 5:6/KJ). Remember the charge of David to his son Solomon, ". . . for the Lord searcheth all hearts, and understandeth all the imaginations of the thoughts; if thou seek him, he will be found of thee; but if thou forsake him, he will cast thee off forever" (I Chronicles 28:9b/KJ).

As we read the Scriptures our spirits are drawn by His Spirit to the awareness of God's love for us. We need to allow Him to move upon our spirits as we feed and meditate on His Word. As we wait upon the Lord and enjoy His presence, He will move in power upon our spirits.

Chapter Eleven
Continuing Our Relationship with God

JESUS SAID, "And you will know the truth, and the truth will set you free" (John 8:32). We need to look back to Calvary constantly to what Christ has already done in our behalf as Christians. Christ has made us free. Our freedom has already been accomplished by our Lord on the cross, paid for nearly 2,000 years ago, and it is our present possession. As we appropriate this and put our complete faith in Him, there is no reason for us to experience the unhappy, fruitless defeat that comes from using our own willpower in our Christian lives. We need to let go of our willpower and completely trust in the Lord. We will then, and only then, experience a victorious Christian life.

We need to read the Bible for our spiritual growth. If we fail in this requirement, our spiritual growth will be stunted. However, forcing ourselves to read the Bible is not a good practice. God says that we should read His Word because we want to. We should read until some nugget of truth is impressed upon us: then stop and meditate upon it. Peter tells us, "Like newborn babies, crave pure spiritual milk, so that by it you may grow up in your salvation, now that you have tasted that the Lord is good" (I Peter 2:2-3/NIV).

Maintaining constant fellowship with God is difficult. A successful prayer life is not out of reach for us. Jesus fasted and prayed after His baptism. Satan tested Him but Jesus appropriated the power of the Holy Spirit within Him and overcame the devil. God is so greatly concerned that we pray that He has promised to answer us when we do. We read His promises over and over in the Bible and we can take Him at His Word. God's Word gives us everything we need to grow in the faith. In Hebrews 11 we read the examples of how God helped many Old Testament saints who lived by faith. What we cannot do for ourselves, God can do for us. However, we must be willing to let Him work in our behalf.

Peter wrote, "Let Him have all your worries and cares, for He is always thinking about you and watching everything that concerns you" (I Peter 5:7). We need to take all our needs to Him — physical, financial, material and spiritual. My husband's favorite verses are in Proverbs. "Trust in the Lord with all your heart, And do not lean on your own understanding. In all your ways acknowledge Him. And He will make your paths straight" (Proverbs 3:5-6/NAS). We also read in Proverbs, "Commit your work to the Lord, then it will succeed" (Proverbs 16:3).

God always draws us to Himself. We need to give ourselves over to His leading and trust Him without reservation. As Job tells us, "But he knows every detail of what is happening to me; and when he has examined me, he will pronounce me completely innocent — as pure as solid gold" (Job 23:10). The Psalmist writes, "For promotion and power come from nowhere on earth, but only from God" (Psalm 75:6). Solomon said, "The mind of man plans his way, But the Lord directs his steps" (Proverbs 16:9/NAS).

The Psalmist said, ". . . No good thing will he withhold from those who walk along his paths" (Psalm 84:11b). David also wrote, "But O my soul, don't be discouraged. Don't be upset. Expect God to act! For I know that I shall again have plenty of reason to praise him for all that he will do. He is my help! He is my God!" (Psalm 42:11).

Through daily confession of our sins, we will receive daily cleansing and we will conquer the sin of prayerlessness. In this way, our fellowship with the Lord will be kept constant.

The power of the flesh is insufficient to develop our prayer life. It seems we always accept God's grace for forgiveness, but many times we neglect to accept His grace for deliverance. When we fail to appropriate His grace for deliverance, we will have a struggle with sin. We must learn to confess our sins, to accept His forgiveness, and then to claim His deliverance. Remember the words spoken by the prophet Zechariah, ". . . Not by might, nor by power, but by my Spirit, says the Lord Almighty — you will succeed because of my Spirit, though you are few and weak" (Zechariah 4:6b).

This well known hymn, *Stand Up, Stand Up for Jesus*, says:

Stand up, stand up for Jesus,
Stand in His strength alone;
The arm of flesh will fail you,
Ye dare not trust your own.
　　　　　　　— George Buffield, Jr.

Pray, Even When It Is Difficult

Sometimes when we go to God in prayer and call
out to Him from the innermost chamber of our
being, we feel like we're talking to Him from a
dark, cold room. All of God's children should
desire to feel and experience the presence of the
Holy Spirit every time they pray, but sometimes
that just doesn't happen. Sometimes when in
prayer we feel cold and weak. The Lord seems to
be far off. Remember what the Lord says: "Stand
silent! Know that I am God!" (Psalm 46:10a). Even
in these times, God is working in our spirit. Our
minds may not comprehend this encounter with
God since we do not feel His power or have the
ability to exercise faith to believe Him. Trust His
promise, ". . . I will never, never fail you nor
forsake you" (Hebrews 13:5b). Remember God is
the one who gave you the desire to pray. He is
drawing you by His Spirit.

When we have a difficult time in prayer, we
must continue to pursue after God. When we do
this, we will grow spiritually as we focus the full
attention of our innermost spirit upon Him Who is
within us. We must not allow restlessness or
anxiety to creep in. The Psalmist has written,
"Don't be impatient! Wait for the Lord, and he will
come and save you! Be brave, stouthearted and
courageous.　Yes,　wait　and　he　will　help　you"

(Psalm 27:14), and "Give your burdens to the Lord. He will carry them. He will not permit the godly to slip or fall" (Psalm 55:22). Remember that the Holy Spirit is within you all the time.

David must have felt like this when suffering the insults of his enemies while in exile. He said, "Take courage, my soul; Do you remember those times (but how could you ever forget them)! When you led a great procession to the Temple on festival days, singing with joy, praising the Lord? Why then be downcast? Why be discouraged and sad?

"Hope in God! I shall yet praise him again. Yes, I shall again praise him for his help. Yet I am standing here depressed and gloomy, but I will meditate upon your kindness. . . But O my soul, don't be discouraged. Don't be upset. Expect God to act! For I know that I shall again have plenty of reason to praise him for all that he will do. He is my help! He is my God!" (Psalm 42:4-6a; 11).

David also prayed, "I am poor and weak, yet the Lord is thinking about me right now! O my God, you are my helper. You are my Savior; come quickly, and save me. Please don't delay!" (Psalm 40:17). In Psalm 66 we read, "Come and hear, all of you who reverence the Lord, and I will tell you what he did for me: For I cried to him for help, with praises ready on my tongue. He would not have listened if I had not confessed my sins. But he listened! He heard my prayer! He paid attention to it! Blessed be God who didn't turn away when I was praying, and didn't refuse me his kindness and love" (Psalm 66:16-20).

When we feel cold and far from God as we seek His face in prayer, we need to do as David did. Sin gives the feeling of coldness and darkness. We

must confess our sin. With unconfessed sin in our
lives, we cannot force God to listen to our prayers
for He will not hear, no matter how hard and
earnestly we pray.

David confessed his sins and rested in the
assurance that God would answer his prayers.
His gloom and discouragement were replaced
with joy and encouragement. He said, "O my soul,
why be so gloomy and discouraged? Trust in God!
I shall again praise him for his wondrous help;
he will make me smile again, for he is my God"
(Psalm 43:5).

We need to keep in mind the admonition of
James, ". . . The earnest prayer of a righteous
man has great power and wonderful results"
(James 5:16b). The prayers of Christians made
righteous in Jesus Christ can have "great power
and wonderful results."

Prayer Warriors As Examples

George Mueller, a well-known man of prayer a
century ago who had an orphanage in London,
England, believed in praying for the daily needs of
all the children who were under his care. He
believed the Lord's words literally, "Give us this
day our daily bread" (Matthew 6:11/KJ). Many
times as they sat down to eat, there was no food on
the table. Still, Mueller would thank God for what
they were about to receive. George Mueller was
"calling those things that be not as though they
were" as Abraham did in Romans 4:17-21.
Against hope, he believed in hope. He was not
weak in faith. He staggered not at God's promise
to supply all his needs. He was fully persuaded

that what God had promised, He would do. And God did answer. Food for those orphans always came when they needed it.

When Jonathan Edwards, a great preacher in the early days of our country, would preach, men would cry out and grab hold of the pillars of their church with their arms for fear they would spend eternity in hell without God. Rev. Edwards wore thick glasses and made awkward gestures while he preached. Many people are unaware that Jonathan Edwards spent anywhere from ten to eighteen hours a day in prayer before he preached a sermon. He was one of the men of God of the period of time in our nation's history known as the "Great Awakening," a time of incredible revival among the people of God.

David Brainerd, a missionary who died at the age of twenty-eight, would prostrate himself in the snow and pray until the snow melted beneath his body. He had a "burning desire" for the Indians to whom he ministered to know Christ.

Andrew Murray wrote a beautiful book entitled *The Prayer Life*. In the book, he speaks of a young missionary, Hudson Taylor, founder of the China Inland Mission (now Overseas Missionary Fellowship). Dr. Taylor had given his entire life over to the control of the Lord. He was convinced he should go to China with the gospel. He had read of the prayer life and great faith of George Mueller and wanted his prayer life to be the same. He knew that before he could have faith to minister in China, he would need to develop and exercise faith in England. He learned that Mueller's great faith was the result of his prayer life.

A modern-day example of how God answers prayer comes from a book entitled *Lord, I Need a Miracle*. In the book is a story of how God answered the prayer of two teenage girls. The girls were leaving a shopping mall after it had closed. When they arrived at their car in the mall parking lot, they saw two men standing nearby with smiles on their faces. They hurried to get into the car, locked the doors and heard the men say, "You won't be going anywhere in that car." The girl driving put the key into the ignition and upon turning it there was nothing, only dead silence.

The young men outside the car told them, "You might as well get out and go with us because the car isn't going to start." As Christians, the two girls held hands and prayed that the Lord would give them a miracle. The driver tried the ignition again, and to the complete amazement of the two young men, the car started and the girls drove away.

When the young ladies arrived home, they told their parents what had happened. Their father was very upset, because just the week before he had had a complete tune-up on the car. He went out to where the car was parked in the driveway, lifted the hood and stood in utter disbelief when he found that the battery was missing. God had answered the girls' prayer. He had given them their miracle. Many times His answers are beyond our comprehension and defy explanation.

God delights in answering the prayers of His children. Andrew Murray states it like this: "Live in the Word — in the love and infinite faithfulness of our Lord Jesus. Even though it is slow and though we may stumble, the kind of faith that always thanks God, not for the experience, but for the promises on which it can rely. That kind of faith goes on from strength to strength, still increasing in the blessed assurance that God Himself will perfect His work in us.

"Our first work ought to be to come into God's presence, not with ignorant prayers, not with many words and thoughts, but in the confidence that the divine work of the Holy Spirit is being carried out within us. This confidence will encourage reverence and quietness. It will also enable us, in dependence on the help the Spirit gives, to lay our desires and heart needs before God. The lesson for every prayer is, see to it first of all, that you commit yourself to the Holy Spirit. And in entire dependence upon Him, give Him first place in your life."

Obedience Brings Answers

God does delight in answering the prayers of His children. The big problem is that there are not too many Christians who are willing to accept His answers and carry out His orders. However, His blessings in our lives will be in direct proportion to our obedience to Him. Since we know that God does delight in answering our prayers, we must dare to believe Him for answers and then exercise the faith to carry out His will.

The Apostles which were at Jerusalem had heard that there were Christians in Samaria. So, Peter and John went to see what had taken place. Soon they realized something was lacking among those Christians there. The Holy Spirit was not overwhelming these new believers. Peter and

John didn't doubt the salvation of the Samaritans but were concerned that the Spirit had not yet fallen upon them. So they laid their hands on them and they received the Holy Spirit (Acts 8:14-17). The Holy Spirit was already indwelling these Samaritan believers. He was ready to overflow but they had to respond, to receive.

This is the first mention of the laying on of hands. The 3,000 at Pentecost, 120 in the upper room, didn't have the laying on of hands to receive the filling and controlling of the Holy Spirit. Peter and John felt it was necessary to lay hands on the Christians in Samaria because they were not rejoicing and praising the Lord as they should, they had not let the Holy Spirit take control.

The Holy Spirit is already living in every Christian. The baptism in the Spirit is not the in-filling, but rather the out-pouring of the Spirit. Upon your salvation, you receive all of the Holy Spirit there is. He is a person. After your salvation experience, pray for the out-flowing, pray for the release. Our problem is that we are not aware of the Spirit at all times, simply because we are in the habit of living from our soul and body.

Let the Holy Spirit motivate you, your feelings, your desires. Let joyful eagerness surface. Never wait for feelings before you begin to do what you know God wants you to do. The Scriptural order is that God blesses you first, then blesses others through you. God's people see God's joy, love and peace in you, then they want to get that joy and peace also.

I have prayed so earnestly that the Lord would enlighten my understanding into the deep things He has for His children. I have asked God, "What is the power of the resurrection that Paul wrote about? What are the things God desires to do for and through His children that are greater than we could ever ask or think? What does it mean when Paul wrote to the Ephesians, '. . . that ye might be filled with all the fullness of God' (Ephesians 3:19b/KJV)? Where is this mighty working power that is to flow from the child of God?" I asked God, "Show me what this 'fullness of God' is that I am to be filled with." It was on my knees in prayer that God began to show me some of the eternal riches of our inheritance in Christ.

God has sent His Spirit to tell us, and His Spirit searches out and shows us all of God's deepest secrets" (I Corinthians 2:10b). And so I prayed, "Lord, by your Spirit, show me what all this means."

Control of the Holy Spirit

The outflowing of the Holy Spirit is different from the receiving of the person of the Holy Spirit when one is born again into the body of Christ. Upon Salvation, the Holy Spirit comes into our lives. He baptizes us into Christ. After having been born into the family of God, the early Apostles were filled and controlled by the Holy Spirit for special ministries. The filling and outflowing of the Holy Spirit is for all who are in Christ. It is part of our inheritance.

Peter said, ". . . Then you also shall receive this gift, the Holy Spirit. For Christ promised Him to each one of you who has been called by the Lord our God, and to your children and even to those in distant lands" (Acts 2:38b-39). We have been called and are therefore "in" on this promise. Praise God!

Have you ever felt starved and hungry spiritually, wondering where the joy was to come from in your life in Christ? The reason believers are so miserable and why we see so little power in our churches today is because we have grieved the Holy Spirit and neglected His power. We will not let the power of God flow through us for fear we might offend. As God said, "The fear of man bringeth a snare" (Proverbs 29:25a/KJ).

Upon salvation you received the Holy Spirit. Now you need to let the Holy Spirit come alive. He is bound in these bodies of ours. We need to release Him and let His power be seen or felt. We must let joy surface and flow out like a river from our innermost being. People will see it and want what we have. Jesus said, "If I be lifted up I will draw all men unto myself" (John 12:32/KJ).

Jesus' last words to His disciples before He ascended up into heaven were, "He that believeth on me, the works that I do shall he do also and greater works than these shall he do because I go to my father. And whatsoever ye shall ask in my name, that will I do that the father may be glorified in the son. If ye ask anything in my name, I will do it" (John 14:12-14/KJ). Isn't that a wonderful promise? Then Paul wrote, "And now just as you trusted Christ to save you, trust Him, too for each day's problems; live in vital union with Him" (Colossians 2:6).

A beautiful quote I have heard is, "The person God will choose to use will be the one who has faith and expects results." If all we ask Him to bless is our food, that is all He will bless. Is His blessing on your food the only request you take into His presence?

We believers have failed to teach and understand what all is included in the inheritance that is ours, that has been bought for us at Calvary. In Galatians we read, "And if ye be Christ's, then are ye Abraham's seed and heirs according to the promise" (Galatians 3:29/KJ). What promise are we heirs to? All God's promises. We're not just heirs of salvation. There is so much more. The key is that we need to have confident assurance, being fully persuaded that whatever we ask the Father in Jesus' Name, according to the will of God, He will do.

Luke, the beloved physician, writes the words of Elizabeth to Mary, the mother of our Lord, "You believed that God would do what He said; that is why He has given you this wonderful blessing" (Luke 2:45). Mary believed God for that which was not humanly possible, simply because God said it would happen. And she conceived and gave birth to the Son of God. She had complete trusting faith.

Jesus grew as a boy into manhood. Things changed in His life when the Holy Spirit came upon Him at His baptism. From that time on, He then exercised His "God power" upon earth to do mighty miracles. He ministered as the God/Man, drawing from the power of God through prayer to perform miracles.

He clearly said, "Believest thou not that I am in the Father, and the Father in me? the words that I speak unto you I speak not of myself: but the Father that dwelleth in me, he doeth the works. Believe me that I am in the Father, and the Father in me: or else believe me for the very works' sake

(John 14:10-11/KJ). Remember He had told them earlier, "I and my Father are one" (John 6:30).

Jesus told His disciples and us, ". . . He that believeth on me, the works that I do shall he do also; and greater works than these shall he do; because I go unto my Father." (John 14:12/KJ).

And knowing their concern of His soon return to His Father, He then instructed them, "And I will pray the Father, and he shall give you another Comforter, that he may abide with you for ever; Even the Spirit of truth; whom the world cannot receive, because it seeth him not, neither knoweth him: but ye know him; for he dwelleth with you, and shall be in you" (John 14:16-17/KJ).

And, dear Christian, with the indwelling Holy Spirit controlling your life, the promise of Jesus will become a living reality in your prayer life: "And whatsoever ye shall ask in my name, that will I do, that the Father may be glorified in the Son. If ye shall ask any thing in my name, I will do it" (John 14:13-14/KJ). Praise God!

Chapter Twelve
Following His Orders

THE MIRACLE of receiving my sight through direct answer to my husband's prayer after thirteen years of blindness took place at 1:00 a.m. on a Saturday morning during our time of prayer before going to bed.

We both began to cry as he prayed with great feeling and boldness: "Oh, God! You can restore Marolyn's eyesight tonight, Lord. I know You can do it! And, God, if it be Your will, I pray You will do it tonight."

Perhaps neither of us was quite prepared for what happened. After 13 blurred and dark years, there was sharpness and light.

"Acie, I can see!" I exclaimed.

"You're kidding," he answered.

I repeated, "I can *see!* I can see the pupils in your eyes!"

Acie thought that perhaps just a little vision had come back.

I said, "Acie, it's 12:30 at night! You need a shave! I can see!"

Acie still couldn't believe the miracle that had really occurred. He grabbed a newspaper, pointed to the large print at the top of the page, and asked, "Can you see this?"

"I can do better than that!" I exclaimed. "I can read the smaller print!"

Acie got excited. "Marolyn, can you see the dresser? Can you see the bed?"

We shouted and praised the Lord for what He had done! Such a miracle was overwhelming. We knew that God was able, but we couldn't comprehend that something so wonderful and miraculous had happened to *us*.

Jumping off the bed, Acie asked the question again, "Marolyn, you can see?"

"Yes!"

"Praise God! Praise God! Praise God! Glory, glory, *glory* to God! It can't be!" Acie exclaimed.

We were beside ourselves with happiness. "This is heaven!" Acie shouted. "It has to be! Oh, God why did I doubt You?"

Then he turned to me, "Why did I doubt God? I didn't believe He could do something like this! He did it!"

We were jumping up and down and crying at the same time. I was getting my *first* look at my husband. For the first time, I could see his face, his eyes, his nose, his mouth. *I could see!*"

I ran to look in the mirror. I could hardly believe how my facial features had changed. I had become blind at 18; now I was 31. I kept taking a second look. . . .

We reached for the phone to call our parents. When the phone rang at my parents' home in Michigan, Mother was awake — she had not been able to sleep that night. For years she had been burdened with the thought of my blindness and her own helplessness in not being able to do anything about it. How happy our news made her! She rejoiced with us over the telephone lines. I asked her to share the news with the others in my family who lived in Holland, Michigan and with my twin sister in New York.

Acie dialed his parents, and his mother sleepily answered. Acie shouted, "Mother, Marolyn can see!" Mom Ford had been awakened in the middle of the night by a son too excited to speak calmly. She asked, "Is everything alright?" But Acie could only repeat over and over: "Marolyn can see! Marolyn can see! She can see!"

That night and all day Saturday were spent in rejoicing and praising God for what He had done. Many of the town's people came to see if what they had heard had really happened. All day I kept saying, "Yes, yes, it's really true. I can see. Hallelujah!"

The next day being Sunday, Acie asked me to share with the congregation of our church how God had restored sight to my blind eyes. Like the man who was born blind whom Jesus healed by the pool of Siloam I simply shared, "'One thing I know, that, whereas I was blind, now I see' (John 9:25b/KJ). Praise God!" It was a glorious Sunday of giving praise to God for His mighty miracle. Over and over I said, "I can see. I can see. I can see! Glory, Hallelujah!"

A couple of weeks later, my husband and I attended a local church's centennial celebration which included dinner on the grounds. As we were eating, the pastor asked if I would share a few words about my miracle with the people of his church. I accepted the opportunity presented, but immediately recalled the days during my growing- up years when I was asked to speak before a group, I would become so fearful my teeth would chatter. As a young girl, I could not speak before a crowd of people. I really wanted to share my testimony and knew that God wanted me to do so.

When it came time for me to speak that day, the Lord took control and He enabled me to speak with such clarity and ease. When the miracle took place, the Lord not only gave sight to my blind eyes, but He also gave me the gift of speaking.

Following the service, ministers of surrounding churches who were there asked me to speak in their churches. After the speaking engagements at those area churches, the various pastors told other pastors about my miracle and what God had done. The number of opportunities to speak grew rapidly.

Some three months later, God called us to serve Him in a church in Arkansas. I thought my speaking engagements would soon be over because the pastors in that area did not know about my miracle. The number of meetings did taper off briefly. Then a lady called me and asked if I would speak at the Arkansas State Southern Baptist Convention Women's Missionary meeting in Little Rock.

At that convention I shared my testimony, followed by a message given by evangelist James Robison. Following the service, Rev. Robison asked if Acie and I would share what the Lord had done for us with the audience of his nationwide telecast.

As a result of that beginning in 1972, it has been my privilege to travel all over the United States, and now I have a world-wide ministry, sharing with multitudes of people the things the Lord has done in my life. He has most graciously provided all that is necessary in my personality, giving me the ability to proclaim His power and wisdom. All that is required of me is my availability and He does the rest.

Having traveled world-wide, the question I am asked most frequently is: "Why did God choose to heal you and not others?"

Examine what God asked Moses as recorded in Exodus: "And the Lord said unto him, 'Who hath made man's mouth? or who maketh the dumb, or deaf, or the seeing, or the blind? have not I the Lord?'" (Exodus 4:11/KJ). God made us as we are for His glory. Remember He is the Potter, we are the clay.

Paul wrote, "But who are you, O man, to talk back to God? Shall what is formed say to him who formed it, 'Why did you make me like this?' Does not the potter have the right to make out of the same lump of clay some pottery for noble purposes and some for common use?" (Romans 9:20-21/NIV).

God says, "The good man does not escape all troubles — he has them too. But the Lord helps him in each and every one." The King James Version words it, "Many are the afflictions of the righteous: but He delivereth them from them all" (Psalm 34:19 - both LB and KJ).

Trials come for different reasons. The Bible teaches that Satan attacks believers. Peter wrote, "Be sober, be vigilant; because your adversary the

devil, as a roaring lion, walketh about, seeking
whom he may devour" (I Peter 5:8/KJ). God says
that Satan comes to kill, to steal and to destroy.
But Jesus tells us that He is come to give us life
and that more abundantly. And John tells us,
"And as Jesus passed by, he saw a man which
was blind from his birth. And his disciples asked
him saying, 'Master, who did sin, this man or his
parents, that he was born blind?' Jesus answered,
'Neither that this man sinned, nor his parents:
but that the works of God should be made manifest
in him'" (John 9:1-3/KJ).

When I had to use a white cane and read Braille
dots, I made the necessary adjustments in my life.
However, Scripture instructs believers to ask God
for a miracle and to pray for healing. James
wrote, "Is any sick among you? let him call for the
elders of the church; and let them pray over him,
anointing him with oil in the name of the Lord:
And the prayer of faith shall save the sick, and the
Lord shall raise him up, and if he have committed
sins, they shall be forgiven him. . . . The effectual
fervent prayer of a righteous man availeth much"
(James 5:14, 15b/KJ). It says that the elders are to
lay hands on the sick person, anoint them with
oil, pray for them, and the sick person shall
recover. God says, "Do it." So we should be
obedient and "do it!"

We must act upon God's Word. Faith is believing
God and knowing He is faithful to keep His
Word. We are not to doubt the Word Jesus gives
us. We must take our eyes off our problems
and circumstances and place them firmly on
Christ. Abraham believed God who ". . . calleth
those things which be not as though they were"

(Romans 4:17b/KJ). Paul continued, "He staggered not at the promise of God through unbelief; but was strong in faith, giving glory to God; And being fully persuaded that, what he had promised, he was able to perform" (Romans 4:20-21/KJ). The Word of God is anointed. It is filled with power. His Word will break every yoke of bondage. In Proverbs we are told that what we meditate on becomes health to our flesh (Proverbs 4:20-22). Faith comes from meditating on the promises. The results come as the Word takes hold in our spirit.

The prophet Hosea wrote, "Come, let us return to the Lord; it is he who has torn us — he will heal us. He has wounded — he will bind us up" (Hosea 6:1). John wrote, "Didn't I tell you that you would see a wonderful miracle from God if you would only believe?" (John 11:40). We, too, will see many wonderful things happen in our lives as we learn to believe God for them.

God says, "My son, attend to my words. Incline thine ear unto my sayings, for they are life to those that find them and health to all thy flesh" (Proverbs 4:20, 22/KJ). "Health" in the Hebrew means "medicine." His Word is "medicine to all our flesh." Don't struggle with unbelief when God has spoken His Word to you. Unspeakable blessings can be yours. Master the difficulties of your prayer life. Break through the sin of limiting God and expect great things from Him. His Word is truth. We read in John, "Ye shall know the truth and the truth shall set you free" (John 8:32/KJ). Paul tells us that we are ". . . more than conquerors through Him who loved us" (Romans 8:37b/KJ).

The Lord says, "My people perish for <u>lack of knowledge</u>" (Hosea 4:6/KJ). We must believe beyond a shadow of a doubt that we have been given authority from God to use the power of the blood of Christ and the power of Jesus' name while here upon earth. It's the positive knowledge of this that is necessary if we are going to break through the cords that hold us captive.

David wrote, "Cast not away therefore your confidence which hath great recompense of reward" (Psalm 45:15/KJ). Paul said, "The word is nigh thee, even in thy mouth — that is the word of faith" (Romans 6:10/KJ). Our confidence held firm is so important. Jesus said, "Whosoever shall say to this mountain; be thou removed and be thou cast into the sea, and shall not doubt in his heart, but shall believe that those things which he saith shall come to pass; and he shall have what he saith" (Mark 11:23/KJ). In Hebrews we read, "Let us hold the profession of our faith without wavering for he is faithful that promised" (Hebrews 10:23/KJ).

In our Christian walk, if we are to grow to spiritual maturity, it is vital we evidence our love for God by our obedience to Him. Remember the words of Jesus, "If ye love me, keep my commandments" (John 14:15/KJ).

The hymn writer has expressed it well:

Trust and obey,
for there's no other way
To be happy in Jesus,
but to trust and obey.

What It Means to Be Born Again

STUDY these Bible verses from God's Word on the subject:

1. "For all have sinned, and come short of the glory of God" (Romans 3:23).

Everyone is a sinner — there are no exceptions.

2. "For the wages of sin is death; but the gift of God is eternal life through Jesus Christ our Lord" (Romans 6:23).

Death means separation forever from God and His love through Jesus Christ.

3. "But God commendeth his love toward us, in that, while we were yet sinners, Christ died for us" (Romans 5:8).

4. "For God so loved the world, that he gave his only begotten Son, that whosoever believeth in him should not perish, but have everlasting life" (John 3:16).

God loved us sinners so much that He gave His Son to die for our sins.

5. "If thou shalt confess with thy mouth the Lord Jesus, and shalt believe in thine heart that God hath raised him from the dead, thou shalt be saved" (Romans 10:9).

189

To be born again, you must believe that Jesus died for your sins, and state publically that you accept Him as Lord of your life.

6.   **"For whosoever shall call upon the name of the Lord shall be saved" (Romans 10:13).**

This is God's promise to you that if you accept Jesus as Lord, He will accept you.

Call upon the Lord now as you pray this prayer:

Dear God, I know I have sinned by breaking Your laws, and I ask for Your forgiveness. I believe that Jesus died for my sins. I want to be born again and receive new life in Him. I will follow Jesus as my Lord and obey Him in all that I do. In the name of Jesus I pray. Amen.

If you pray this prayer to receive Christ as your personal Savior, please write me and let me know of your decision.

Marolyn Ford
6083 Surrey Hollow Cove
Memphis, TN 38134

Bibliography

Prayer Changes Things by Charles Allen. Spire Press, 1974.

All Things Are Possible Through Prayer by Charles Allen. Fleming H. Revell, Publisher.

The Weapon of Prayer by E. M. Bounds. Baker Book House, 1975.

Purpose In Prayer by E. M. Bounds. Moody Press Publication.

The Power of Prayer by Thomas Elliff. Broadman Press, 1977.

Reece Howell: Intercessor by Norman Grubb. Christian Literature Crusade, 1952.

Prayer by O. Hallensby. Augsburg Publishing House, 1931.

Heavens Of Brass by Rick Ingle. Heavens of Brass, Inc., 1974.

The Ministry of Intercession by Andrew Murray. Whitaker House, 1982.

The Prayer Life by Andrew Murray. Moody Press.

The Spiritual Man by Watchman Nee. Christian Fellowship Publishers, 1977.

Drawn by His Love by Jerry Savelle. Harrison House, 1987.

Enduring to the End (Tape) by Dr. Mary Stewart Relfe. League of Prayer, Inc.